Managing India's Services Exports

Har Sandeep Kaur

ATLANTIC
PUBLISHERS & DISTRIBUTORS (P) LTD

Published by
ATLANTIC
PUBLISHERS & DISTRIBUTORS (P) LTD
7/22, Ansari Road, Darya Ganj, New Delhi-110002
Phones : +91-11-40775252, 23273880, 23275880, 23280451
Fax : +91-11-23285873
Web : www.atlanticbooks.com
E-mail : orders@atlanticbooks.com

Branch Office
5, Nallathambi Street, Wallajah Road, Chennai-600002
Phones : +91-44-64611085, 32413319
E-mail : chennai@atlanticbooks.com

Printed in India at Nice Printing Press, A-33/3A, Site-IV, Industrial Area, Sahibabad, Ghaziabad, U.P.

have been possible without the guidance and the help of several individuals who in one way or another contributed and extended their valuable assistance in the preparation and completion of this study.

First and foremost, above all my greatest regards to the Almighty for bestowing the courage to face the complexities of life and complete this project.

I am eternally grateful to Prof. Jaswinder Singh Brar, Centre for Research in Eeconomic Change, Department of Economics, Punjabi University, Patiala for his excellent guidance and continuous support. This work would not have been possible without his guidance, constant support, and encouragement. His precious advice, motivation, immense knowledge, and valuable discussion helped me a lot in completion of this project.

I am equally thankful to Dr. G.S. Batra, the Head, School of Management Studies, for his support and valuable guidance. I would like to express my sincere gratitude to Indian Council of Social Science Research (ICSSR), New Delhi for providing me research fellowship and financial support to complete this project.

I would like to thank my family, especially my mother who raised me with love and supported me in all my pursuits. Words are inadequate in offering my thanks to my younger brother Kanwar Iqbal Singh Bhangoo for his support.

Har Sandeep Kaur

Contents

List of Tables

List of Figures

List of Abbreviations

AAAES	Average Annual Adjusted Export Share
AAOES	Average Annual Observed Export Share
AES	Adjusted Export Share
ASEAN	Association of South East Asian Nations
ASIDE	Assistance to States for Developing Export Infrastructure and Allied Activities
ANZCERT	Australia-New Zealand Closer Economic Relations Trade Agreement
BIMSTEC	Bay of Bengal Initiative for Multi-Sectoral Technical and Economic Cooperation
BPO	Business Process Outsourcing
BRICS	Brazil, Russia, India, China, South Africa
CAGR	Compound Annual Growth Rate
CBSE	Central Board of Secondary Education
CEP	Comparative Export Performance
ELG	Export-Led Growth
EU	European Union
FDI	Foreign Direct Investment
FER	Foreign Exchange Rate
FTA	Free Trade Agreement
GATT	General Agreement on Trade and Tariffs
GATS	General Agreement on Trade in Services
GDP	Gross Domestic Product
GoI	Government of India

GNI	Gross National Income
HDI	Human Development Index
HRD	Human Resource Development
IT	Information Technology
J&K	Jammu and Kashmir
MAI	Market Access Initiative
MERCOSUR	Spanish: Mercado Común del Sur
MDA	Market Development Assistance
OECD	Organisation for Economic Cooperation and Development
OES	Observed Export Share
OF	Openness Factor
OPEC	Organisation of Petroleum Exporting Countries
RBI	Reserve Bank of India
RCA	Revealed Comparative Advantage
R&D	Research and Development
SAARC	South Asian Association for Regional Cooperation
SATIS	SAARC Agreement on Trade In Services
SEZs	Special Economic Zones
SMEs	Small and Medium-sized Enterprises
TEE	Towns of Export Excellence
TGR	Trend Growth Rate
UK	United Kingdom
UN	United Nations
UNCPC	United Nations Central Product Classification
UNCTAD	United Nations Conference on Trade and Development
USA	United States of America
USSR	Union of Soviet Socialist Republics
WEF	World Economic Forum
WTO	World Trade Organisation

Chapter 1

Services Trade: Introduction

1.1 Introduction

International trade in services during the era of globalisation, liberalisation, and privatisation has set new nexus between economic growth and growth of exports of services. This phenomenon has been prevailing in most of the countries, especially in developing and emerging economies including India. Growth of exports of services has been the main driving force behind high economic growth trajectory of India during the recent past. Further, during neoliberal policy regime in India around 90 per cent of the economic growth has been explained by the tertiary sector (Banga and Kumar, 2010). Indian economy experienced changes in sectoral distribution of gross domestic product (GDP) due to the increasing contribution of service sector under the new economic dispensation. In India, the growth of service sector is almost along the global service market trends during neo-liberal regime, but there are two distinctive features of this growth firstly, the entire decline in the share of primary sector in GDP has been absorbed by the service sector and share of manufacturing remained the same. Secondly, in spite of the rising share of services in GDP and trade, there has not been a corresponding rise in the share of services in total employment, which has raised doubts about its sustainability (Banga, 2005).

1.2 Structure of Indian Economy: GDP Distribution and Growth

The study of structural changes over the period of time and structure of the economy are of paramount importance to gauge the economic growth and performance of any economy. In this light, an attempt has been made to analyse the sectoral distribution and growth of India's GDP during 1950-51 to 2011-12 period. For this purpose, the period 1950-51 to 2011-12 has been divided into five different sub-periods on the basis of changing economic policy and development strategy. Firstly, Nehruvian-Mahalanobis strategy era from 1950-51 to 1964-65, during this period growth strategy coincided with implementation of constitution, five year planning, industrial policy based on the development of basic and heavy industries. This strategy consisted of three main aspects of development and laid emphasis on fulfillment of these aspects. These included (a) developing a sound base for initiating the process of long-term growth, (b) a high priority to industrialization and finally, (c) emphasis on development of capital goods industries (Mahalanobis, 1953). Second from 1965-66 to 1979-80, the period of industrial deceleration, green revolution and agricultural led-growth strategy. Third from 1980-81 to 1991-92, the period of starting of liberalisation and fulfillment of minimum needs-led growth strategy. Fourth sub-period from 1992-93 to 2001-02, the economic reforms and structural adjustment programme led-growth strategy era and finally the post-economic reforms period from 2002-03 to 2011-12. The information regarding the sectoral distribution and growth of GDP of five sub-periods has been shown in Table 1.1.

The analysis shows that during Nehruvian-Mahalanobis development growth strategy era based upon heavy and basic industries and public sector led growth that share of primary sector has declined from about 55 per cent to 47.1 per cent in India's GDP. The share of secondary sector during the same period increased from about 15 per cent to over 20 per cent and share of tertiary sector also increased from about 30 per cent to 32.5 per cent of the GDP. This period witnessed the adoption

Table 1.1: Percentage Distributions and Growth of GDP, 1950-1951 to 2011-12

(2004-05 Constant Prices)

Year	Primary Sector[1]	Secondary Sector[2]	Tertiary Sector[3]	Total[4]
Period I (1950-51 to 1964-65): Nehruvian-Mahalanobis-led Growth Strategy				
1950-51 to 1952-53	54.9	14.8	30.3	100
1953-54 to 1955-56	54.6	15.5	29.9	100
1956-57 to 1958-59	52.3	17.0	30.7	100
1959 -60 to 1961-62	50.4	18.4	31.2	100
1962-63 to 1964-65	47.1	20.4	32.5	100
1950-51 to 1964-65 TGR[5]	**2.7**	**6.8**	**4.6**	**3.9**
Period II (1965-66 to 1979-80): Industrial Deceleration and Agriculture-led Growth Strategy				
1965-66 to 1967-68	43.8	22.1	34.1	100
1968-69 to 1970-71	44.1	22.1	33.8	100
1971-72 to 1973-74	42.4	22.3	35.2	100
1974-75 to 1976-77	41.5	22.2	36.2	100
1977-78 to 1979-80	39.3	23.6	37.1	100
1965-66 to 1979-80 TGR[5]	**2.6**	**4.1**	**4.4**	**3.6**
Period III (1980-81 to 1991-92): Liberalisation and Minimum Needs-led Growth Strategy				
1980-81 to 1982-83	38.3	23.3	38.4	100
1983-84 to 1985-86	37.2	23.2	39.6	100
1986-87 to 1988-89	34.3	23.5	42.2	100
1989-90 to 1991-92	32.9	24.0	43.2	100
1980-81 to 1991-92 TRG[5]	**3.4**	**5.6**	**6.7**	**5.2**

Period IV (1992-93 to 2001-02): SAP and Economic Reforms-led Growth Strategy				
1992-93 to 1994-95	31.7	23.7	44.6	100
1995-96 to 1997-98	28.7	25.0	46.3	100
1998-99 to 2000-01	26.3	24.1	49.7	100
1992-93 to 2001-01 TRG[5]	**3.3**	**6.8**	**8.4**	**6.5**
Period V (2001-02 to 2011-02): Post-Economic Reforms Era				
2001-02	25.2	23.7	51.1	100
2002-03	23.1	24.4	52.5	100
2003-04	23.2	24.4	52.4	100
2004-05	21.9	25.1	53.0	100
2005-06	20.9	25.3	53.7	100
2006-07	20.0	26.1	54.0	100
2007-08	19.3	26.3	54.4	100
2008-09	18.1	25.8	56.1	100
2009-10	16.9	26.0	57.1	100
2010-11	16.8	25.7	57.5	100
2011-12	16.5	26.1	57.4	100
2001-02 to 2011-12 TRG[5]	**3.6**	**9.2**	**9.5**	**8.2**

Note: 1. Primary Sector—Agriculture, forestry and fishing, mining and quarrying, 2. Secondary Sector—Manufacturing, construction, electricity, gas and water supply, 3. Tertiary Sector—Trade, hotels, transport and communication, financing, insurance, real estate and business services, community, social and Personal services, 4. Total—(1+2+3) 5. TGR—Trend Growth Rate

Source: Economic Survey 2013-14, Ministry of Finance, Government of India.

of constitution, initiation of long-term planned economic development and industrial policy resolution 1956 and public sector-led economic development. These developments have resulted in low growth rate of 2.7 per cent of primary sector and higher growth rates of 6.8 per cent of secondary sector and 4.6 per cent of tertiary sector during the period. The growth of GDP during this period has registered growth rate of 3.9 per cent. It is clear from the analysis that the decline in the share of primary sector in GDP has been more absorbed by secondary sector as compared to tertiary sector.

The analysis shows that during the period of industrial deceleration and adoption of agriculture-led growth strategy, the share of primary sector has decreased from 43.8 per cent to 39.3 per cent of the GDP. The shares of secondary sector and tertiary sector over the same period have increased from 22.1 per cent to 23.6 per cent and 34.1 per cent to 37.1 per cent respectively of the GDP. It is pertinent to mention that this period witnessed an Indo-Pak war, first oil shock and enforcement of emergency in the country. Therefore, these developments and deceleration of industrial growth have led the policy-makers to adopt agriculture-led growth strategy to cope up with the economic problems of the country. During this period, the growth rate of GDP was 3.6 per cent and sectoral growth rates were 2.6 per cent, 4.1 per cent and 4.4 per cent of primary, secondary and tertiary sector respectively. It is also evident from the analysis that during this period decline in the share of primary sector in the GDP has been more absorbed by tertiary sector as compared to secondary sector.

During liberalisation and adoption of minimum needs-led growth strategy period, the share of primary sector decreased from 38.3 per cent to 32.9 per cent of the GDP. The shares of secondary sector and tertiary sector on the other hand increased from 23.3 per cent to 24.0 per cent and 38.4 per cent to 43.2 per cent respectively of the GDP over the same period. This period witnessed political instability and uncertainty as well as major changes in the economic and industrial policy of the country. In spite of this, the growth rate of GDP has remained comparatively high at 5.2 per cent and sectoral growth rates were 3.4 per cent, 5.6 per cent and 6.7 per cent of primary, secondary and tertiary sector, respectively during the period. Again, it is clear from the analysis that during this period the tertiary sector has gained more as compared to secondary sector of the decline of primary sector's share in the GDP.

Structural adjustment programme and economic reforms-led growth strategy era during 1990s saw major changes in the economic policy as Indian economy has been opened up for foreign investors. Liberalisation, globalisation, and privatisation policies have resulted in stagnation of primary sector as its growth rate remained same at 3.3 per cent and share in GDP declined from about 32 per cent to 26 per cent, but overall GDP registered a high growth rate of 6.5 per cent. However, secondary and tertiary sectors have registered high growth rates of 6.8 per cent and 8.4 per cent respectively during the period. Further, the share of secondary sector in GDP remained the same and the entire decline of primary sector has been absorbed by the tertiary sector as its share increased from about 45 per cent to 50 per cent of the GDP during the period.

The share of primary sector in GDP has sharply declined from about 25 per cent to 17 per cent and its growth rate remained stagnated during the post-economic reforms period. However, the share of secondary sector has increased from about 24 per cent to 26 per cent of the GDP with high annual growth rate of 9.2 per cent. The tertiary sector has mainly absorbed the sharp decline of primary sector as the share of tertiary has increased from about 51 per cent to 57 per cent in GDP with 9.5 per cent growth rate during the same period. During this period, the overall annual growth of GDP remained at 8.2 per cent and tertiary sector become the leading sector of the Indian economy.

Above analysis clearly suggests that over the period of time due to changing economic policies the structure of Indian economy has experienced major shifts. The primary sector stagnated and its share in GDP has declined sharply and secondary sector gained less as compared to tertiary sector. Presently, the tertiary sector has been the major deriver of the growth of Indian economy. Further, the share of export of services in the total exports of India has been increasing over the years. Therefore, Indian service exports are not only of importance in India's overall international trade but are also as an important component of overall national economic growth. Among all the countries, in 2010, India ranked 10th from above in the exports of services and 20th in merchandised exports. Reforms in the trade policy of India have identified trade in services as a key and strategic sector under the export-led growth strategy. Government of India attempts to exploit the opportunities of trade in services and has setup a Service Export Promotion Council for the purpose. Further, policy also provides exemptions on taxes on many exportable services. Therefore, it is of paramount importance to investigate the various dimensions of growing of service exports of the country.

1.3 Trade in Services: Theory and Concepts

Theories of trade especially theory of comparative costs based on the concept of opportunity cost and new theory of trade based on the competitive advantage of specilisation have also been applied to explain the international trade in services. The debate over the application of these theories to international trade in services has divided the experts into three groups on the basis of location of production of services, consumption, accumulation and inventory and transportability. Firstly, Hindley and Smith (1984), Hindley (1990), and Sapir and Winter (1994) have argued that in the absence of any theory of trade in services and under perfect competition conditions these theories of trade also explain the trade in services as well. Secondly, Hill (1977) objected to the application of these theories to trade in services and argued that goods and services belonged to different categories. Further, the services cannot be stored and accumulated, rather instantly consumed, and argued that same location of production and consumption of services for essential interaction of user and provider of services. Finally, Bhagwati (1984 and 1985), Melvin (1987 and 1989), Stern and Hoekman (1988), and Hoekman and Braga (1997) have put the arguments that services can be divided into many categories, some requires same location of production and consumption and others do not require this proximity, therefore argued different interpretation for the theory of trade in services. Therefore, in such a situation, the concepts of trade in services and theoretical framework as provided by Sampson and Snape (1985) and modified by Sapir and Winter (1994) and adopted under the General Agreement on Trade in Services (GATS) by World Trade Organisation (WTO) have been used in the present study. These supply-based four modes are as follows.

According to GATS, the tradability of services has been divided on the basis of mode of delivery into four categories (United Nations, 2002). Firstly, Cross Border Mode, i.e. services supplied from one country to another with the buyer and seller staying at their respective locations. Management consultancy services, marketing services, health services, education and training and transportation services are included in this mode. Secondly, Consumption Abroad Mode relates to the services provided to nationals of another country bringing the buyer to the location of the seller. Tourism and travel-related services, education and training; legal services and health care services are the important mode of this category. Thirdly, Commercial Presence Mode refers to the presence of seller at the buyer's location by setting up subsidiaries/branches to provide services in other countries. Financial services, engineering and construction services, information technology services, and distribution services constitute this category. Finally, Movement of Natural Person's Mode relates to individuals moving to the location of the buyer. Art and cultural services, construction services, education and training services, environmental services, geometrics services and recreational and sporting services fall under this mode.

1.4 Objectives of the Study

The specific objectives of the study are as follows:

(a) to study the growth and trends of exports of services of India;

(b) to study the composition and direction of export of services of India;

(c) to study the global competitiveness and performance of India in the export of services;

(d) to examine the major determinants of India's export of services;

(e) to identify the major managerial and policy issues impacting India's service exports; and

(f) to suggest suitable policy measures for further strengthening of exports of services.

1.5 Hypotheses

The study intends to examine the following hypotheses:

1. India's services exports performed well than that of other suppliers in world market.
2. India's services exports were affected by four major determinants, namely size of economy, technology, human development and international capital movement.

1.6 General Approach, Methodology and Data Base

During the post-WTO and GATS regime dominance of services in national income and national exports of the country has been witnessed. The country has also been emerging a strong player of exports of services in the world. Keeping this in view, the present study intends to examine the various dimensions of services exports of India. The analysis would be confined to the post-WTO period, i.e. January 1995, because it provides the comprehensive framework for the international trade in services. Therefore, the study would cover the period from 1995 to 2012. However, due to the inclusion and classification of services in different years differently, from 1980 to 1999 the services were classified into three categories as (1) transport, (2) travel, and (3) other services. From the year 2000 the services were classified into twelve categories along with codes as (01) transport, (02) travel, (05) other services, (07) communications, (06) construction, (16) insurance, (13) financial services, (10) computer and information services, (14) royalties and license fees, (15) other business services, (18) personal, cultural and recreational services, and (21) government services (UNCTAD, 2014).

In the above scenario, the present study would cover the service category wise brief analysis from 1995-99 and from 2000 to 2012 deeper and wider service category wise analysis has been conducted. The time series data pertaining to the chosen period for the relevant services, countries and other economic variables will provide the necessary foundation to the analysis and hence study. The study is entirely based on secondary data.

The main sources of data are: (a) Reserve Bank of India (RBI); (b) Organisation for Economic Cooperation and Development (OECD); (c) World Trade Organisation (WTO); (d) Ministry of Trade and Commerce; (e) United Nations Conference on Trade And Development (UNCTAD); and (f) World Bank and various others institutions and agencies.

The data and information related to various services was processed and analysed by applying various relevant statistical methods, tests and techniques. The real growth in services has been ascertained by using the trend growth rates (TGRs) and for purpose the following equation has been applied and used to calculate TGR wherever applicable.

Trend Growth Rate:

Let the equation be

$$Y = ab^t \qquad \text{...(1.1)}$$

Where, Y is the concerned variable

t is the time variable

b = (1 + r); where 'r' is growth rate

'a' and 'b' are constants

taking log on both sides of equation 1.1

$$\log Y = \log a + t \log b \qquad \text{...(1.2)}$$

Equation 1.2, a semi-log equation will be estimated by running regression, log y on t, so 'log a' and 'log b' will be estimated.

The trend growth rate 'r' is estimated by taking anti-log of estimated parameter log b, attached to time variable in the semi-log equation and subtracting one from it and multiplying the residual by 100.

Observed Export Share (OES) index is used in order to calculate the share of Indian services exports in world services exports. In this index, India's share of service exports in world's exports of services is determined. Adjusted Export Share (AES) index is being used to overcome the limitation of effect of a country's size of economy on its services exports, in this case India. In this index, the degree of export concentration of India's services export in degree of export concentration of world's services export is measured. Openness Factor (OF) index is then used in the study in order to investigate a country's dependency on a particular service by taking into accounts both the imports and exports of that particular service (Peterson and Barras, 1987). To study India's competitiveness and performance of exports of services we applied two broadly used indices, firstly, the Balassa Index (Balassa, 1965) or revealed comparative advantage (RCA), on the basis of a India's specialisation in exports relative to the world, BRICS and SAARC countries, one of the most widely used methods. Secondly, similarly the comparative export performance (CEP) index applied to measure comparative advantage of India's exports relative to the world, BRICS and SAARC countries, it is a slightly modified version of the Balassa Index and measures the export specialisation of a country for particular product. The regression technique will be used to investigate the major determinants of services exports of India. Four main determinants have been identified in the study and their effect on exports of services of India has been calculated using this technique. The resultant information would be presented by using the appropriate tabular systems and methods.

❐

Chapter 2

Services Sector of India: Theoretical Issues

2.1 Introduction

International trade theories based on the comparative cost approach and the specialisation approach explain the patterns of trade between the countries. The applicability of both these approaches for evaluating international trade in services, its competitiveness and performance are of paramount importance (Peterson and Barras, 1987). In economic literature, the opinion and views regarding the application of these theories to international trade in services has been divided. The main objections for the application international trade theories to trade in services raised were that goods and services belong to different categories, as services are a flow and cannot be stored and accumulated and for trade in services the same location of production and consumption of services is required, i.e. the proximity of suppliers and consumers (Hill, 1977). Therefore, due to the need for proximity in international trade in services, certain factors like distance place a cost burden on certain forms of services delivery hindered the services trade across the borders (Francois and Hoekman, 2010). But it has also been argued that services can be divided into many categories, some requires same location of production and consumption and other services do not require such proximity (Bhagwati, 1984; Braga, 1997). However, many argued that in the absence of any specific theory of trade in services these theories of trade also explain the trade in services (Hindley, 1990; Sapir and Winter, 1994).

The comparative cost-based approach suggests that relative cost differences in inputs and outputs between countries arise due to natural resources, labour, state policies, capital, institutions, skill levels and technology and it makes trade between countries possible and feasible (Copeland and Mattoo, 2008). Also, these factors and variables have been identified and considered determinants of exports of services. The specialisation approach suggests that countries also exploit their competitiveness/ specialisation in producing certain goods and services (Peterson and Barras, 1987). Along with these approaches of international trade managerial decisions, perceptions, opinions and perspectives regarding brand image, innovations, export promotion strategy, foreign market characteristics and other issues were also be believed to be determinants of export performance (Lages et al., 2005). In this scenario, exports of the countries are dominated by specialized goods and services. Therefore, the international trade in services has been guided by comparative cost of production, specialisation in production and managerial perspectives. In this chapter, an attempt has been made to study the classification and supply modes of services, India's services trade policy and trade agreements in services. This chapter has been structured into six sections. Introduction to the theory of international trade has been discussed in section 2.1. The international and Indian classification and governance of services has been listed in section 2.2. The supply modes of providing services at different locations has been analysed in section 2.3. Issues of managerial perspective, services trade policy and issues and services trade agreements have been analysed in section 2.4, section 2.5 and section 2.6 respectively. The emerging conclusions from the analysis have been presented in the final section of the chapter.

2.2 Services Sector of India: Governance and Classification

Indian federalism, under the Constitution of India, since its inception has been striving to improve the material well-being of the Indian citizens, for the purpose the country has embarked on comprehensive socio-economic policy and planning pervading all aspects of national life. This has necessitated a complete mobilization of country's resources to develop and to take care of the industry, agriculture, land reforms, population, exploitation of natural resources and provisions of social services as education, health, housing, business, transport, travel and others (Jain, 1968). Due to the federal governance structure of India, the division, governance and classification of service sector of India have been under the jurisdiction of Central Government, State Governments and in some cases jointly by Central and State Governments (Mukherjee, 2013). Therefore, service sector and international trade in services of India has been regulated and controlled by the multiple ministries and agencies of Central and State Governments. Here an attempt has been made to understand and locate the jurisdiction of various services under the federal governance structure of India. The jurisdictions in the service sector have been given below:

(a) Union List: The Constitution of India puts the telecommunication, postal, broadcasting, financial services such as insurance and banking, national highways, mining services under the jurisdiction and governance of Central Government.

(b) State List: The Constitution of India provides the jurisdiction and governance of health care and related services, real estate services, retail services, agriculture services, hunting and forestry to State Governments.

(c) Concurrent List: Professional services, education, printing and publishing, and electricity services have been under the jurisdiction and governance of Centre and State Governments.

Further, the services and service sector can also be classified on the basis of industrial policy classification and national industrial classification. But, for international comparisons and trade in services negotiations the classification provided by the United Nations Central Product Classification (UNCPC) has been used. In the present analysis, an attempt has been made to provide both classifications of service sector and services, National Industrial Classification and UNCPC under GATT and GATS. Firstly, The National Industrial Classification, 2008 has been presented below:

Section G: Wholesale and retail trade; repair of motor vehicles.

Section H: Transportation and storage.

Section I: Accommodation and Food Service Activities.

Section J: Information and Communication.

Section K: Financial and Insurance Activities.

Section L: Real Estate Activities.

Section M: Professional, Scientific and Technical Activities.

Section N: Administrative and Support Service Activities.

Section O: Public administration and defense; compulsory social security.

Section P: Education.

Section Q: Human Health and Social Work Activities.

Section R: Arts, Entertainment and Recreation.

Section S: Other Service Activities.

Section T: Activities of households as employers; undifferentiated goods and services producing activities of households for own use.

Section U: Activities of extraterritorial organisations and bodies.

Secondly, at the international level services sector and international trade in services have been classified as traditional services under the GATT and modern/professional services under the GATS. Here, the services classification under GATT up to 1999 also known as traditional classification has been presented below:

(a) Transport services,

(b) Travel services,

(c) Other services, and

(d) Total services.

Table 2.1: Details of Classifications of Services by UNCTAD

Service Code	Services	Description
01	Transport services: 01	Covers all transportation services that involve carriage of passengers, movement of goods (freight), rentals with crew, and related supporting services. Excludes freight insurance, which is included with insurance services. Excludes goods procured in ports by non-resident carriers and repairs on transport equipment, which are included in goods.
02	Travel services: 02	Includes goods and services acquired from an economy by non-resident travellers during visits shorter than one year.
05	Other services: 05	Includes all service categories expect transport and travel.
07	Communication services: 07	Consists of postal, courier and telecommunications services between residents and non-residents.
06	Construction services: 06	Covers the work performed on construction projects and installations by an enterprise outside the economy of residence of that enterprise.
16	Insurance services: 16	Covers all types of insurance, reinsurance and related auxiliary services. Insurance services are estimated or valued by the service charges included in total premiums rather than by total value of the premiums.

13	Financial services: 13	Included financial intermediation and auxiliary services, except those directly related to life insurance and pension funds (covered under insurance services).
10	Computer and Information services: 10	(a) Computer services consist of hardware and software-related services and data processing. (b) New agency services include the provision of news, photographs and feature articles to the media. (c) Other information services cover database services: database conception, data storage and dissemination of data. Direct non-bulk subscriptions to periodicals regardless of means of information transmission also belong to this service category.
14	Royalties and License Fees services: 14	Covers franchising fees, royalties paid for the use of registered trademarks, and other fees paid for authorised use of intangible, non-produced non-financial assets and proprietary rights. Distributive rights with limitations for audiovisual products are not included here.
15	Other Business services: 15	Includes merchandising and other trade-related services; operational leasing services; and miscellaneous business, professional and technical services (legal, advertising, consultancy, accounting, R&D, etc.)

18	Personal, Cultural and Recreational services: 18	(a) Audiovisual and related services cover the production of motion pictures; video and radio programmes, musical readings, (and similar) including fees paid to personnel involved. Related limited distribution rights are also covered. Fees paid for sporting, theatrical and similar events belong to this category as well. (b) Other personal, cultural and recreational services encompass services associated with museums, libraries, archives, and other cultural and sporting activities. Education and health services are covered under this category (excluding, however, the expenses for health and education services paid by travellers, which belong to travel services).
21	Government services: 21	Residual category covering government (embassies, consulates, military units, etc.) transactions in goods and services not included in other categories. It also covers the transactions of international organisations.

Source: UNCTAD, 2014

After the establishment of GATS under WTO agreements by the member countries in 1995, the new, modern/professional classification of services has been introduced and adopted by UNCTAD from 2000 onwards. The details of this new classification of services by UNCTAD have been presented in Table 2.1.

The analysis of service sector governance and classification of services suggests that though, at the national level and international level widespread differences have been observed in the case of division, classification and governance, there are also some commonalities and similarities in the classification of service sector. In case of governance of services, Indian Government has clearly divided the jurisdiction of services among Central Government, State Government and in some services both Central and State Governments. Classification of services on the other hand is not as clearly specified and international classification by UNCTAD under GATS includes 12 categories of services. On the national level the National Industrial Classification of 2008 given by Indian Government divides services into 15 categories with some common and some different categories. Therefore, there is a need for a new and well defined and comprehensive classification of services that could be followed internationally by all the countries.

2.3 Services in International Trade: Supply Modes of Services

The concepts of trade in services and theoretical framework as provided by Sampson and Snape (1985) and modified by Sapir and Winter (1994) and adopted under the General Agreement on Trade in Services (GATS) by World Trade Organisation (WTO) have been used in the present study. According to General Agreement on Trade in Services (GATS), the tradability of services has been divided on the basis of mode of delivery into four categories (United Nations, 2002). These supply based four modes have been presented in Table 2.2.

Firstly, Cross Border Mode, i.e. services supplied from one country to another with the buyer and seller staying at their respective locations. Management consultancy services, marketing services, health services, education and training and transportation services are included in this mode. Secondly, Consumption Abroad Mode relates to the services provided to nationals of another country bringing the buyer to the location of the seller. Tourism and travel-related services, education and training; legal services and health care services are the important mode of this category. Thirdly, Commercial Presence Mode

Table 2.2: Supply Modes of Services According to GATS

Mode		Description
Mode 1	Cross-border trade	Supply of a service from the territory of one member into that of another member, i.e., supplier and consumer interact across distance.
Mode 2	Consumption abroad	Consumption of a service by consumers of one member who have moved into the territory of the supplying member.
Mode 3	Commercial presence	Services are provided by foreign suppliers that are commercially established in the territory of another member.
Mode 4	Presence of natural persons	Services are supplied by foreign natural persons, either employed or self-employed, who currently stay in the territory of another member.

Source: Compiled from Mattoo, Aaditya et al., 2008

refers to the presence of seller at the buyer's location by setting up subsidiaries/branches to provide services in other countries. Financial services, engineering and construction services, information technology services, and distribution services constitute this category. Finally, Movement of Natural Person's Mode relates to individuals moving to the location of the buyer. Art and cultural services, construction services, education and training services, environmental services, geometrics services and recreational and sporting services fall under this mode.

2.4 Services Exports of India: Managerial Issues

Marketing mix or export marketing strategy based on four Ps includes promotion, place, product and price has been considered as major determinant of exports (Borden, 1964; Lages et al., 2005; Moghaddam et al., 2011). There are mainly two approaches of marketing mix firstly, relating to goods known as Product Marketing Mix and secondly, related to services known as Services Marketing Mix or extended marketing mix. The Product Marketing Mix consists of four Ps called product, price, place and promotions and the Services Marketing Mix includes seven Ps and three additional variables included are people, physical evidence and process to the four Ps. In the present study, an attempt has been made to analyse these issues of marketing mix and export marketing strategy especially extended marketing mix in detail and the analysis and discussion regarding this has been presented below. Services marketing mix frame work has be presented in Table 2.3, Table 2.4 and Figure 2.1.

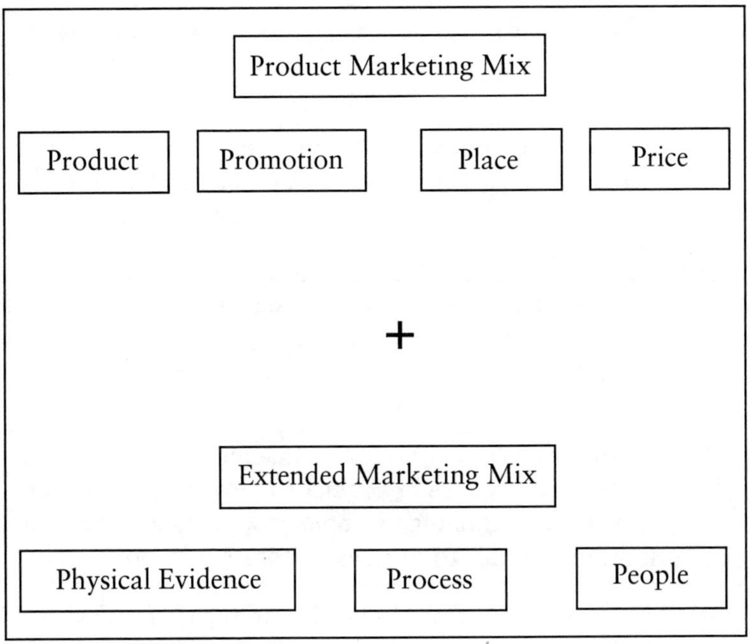

Figure 2.1: Services Marketing Mix Seven Ps Approach

Source: Christopher Lovelock and Jochen Wirtz, 2004

Table 2.3: Services Marketing Mix/Extended Marketing Mix Model

1.	Price marketing strategy: low-cost advantage, price competitiveness/value, adjustment of export prices to foreign market situation, pricing strategy, sales terms, credit policy, currency strategy, price adaption.
2.	Promotion marketing strategy: investment in promotional activity, advertising and trade promotion, advertising expenditure, sale promotion, personal selling, trade fairs.
3.	Place marketing strategy: export channel type, distribution strategy, dealer support, direct exporting channel, distribution network, distribution channel, availability.
4.	Product marketing strategy: product design, quality and services, brand image, product differentiation, product innovation, packaging and labelling.
5.	Physical environment marketing strategy: create and maintain physical appearances, buildings, interior designs, well-dressed staff, sounds and smell and other tangibles.
6.	Process marketing strategy: design of activity flows, promoters of value chain components, nature of customers' involvement, role of contact personnel, role of technology, degree of automation.
7.	People marketing strategy: managing the human side of the enterprise, right contact employees, recruitment, selection and training of employees, right customers for firm, firm is able to manage customer behaviour.

Source: 1. Moghaddam et al., 2011, 2. Christopher Lovelock and Jochen Wirtz, 2004

Table 2.4: Significant Dimensions of Marketing Mix Strategy Proposed in Literature

Determinates of Export Performance	Study/Years	Dimensions of Strategy
Product Marketing Strategy	(a) Tantong et al. (2010) (b) Lages et al. (2009) (c) Mavrogiannis et al. (2008)	(a) Product design adaption strategy (b) Product innovation, product quality (c) Product design, brand mix, warranty, after sales services
Promotion Marketing Strategy	(a) Eusebio et al. (2007) (b) Lee and Griffith (2004) (c) Leonidou et al. (2002)	(a) Commercial branch in export market (b) Advertising, trade promotion, advertising expenditure (c) Sale promotion, personal selling, trade fairs, personal visit
Place Marketing Strategy	(a) Eusebio et al. (2007) (b) Lee and Griffith (2004) (c) Leonidou et al. (2002)	(a) Own centres (b) Direct exporting channel (c) Dealer support, export sales representative office and direct purchasing
Price Marketing Strategy	(a) Eusebio et al. (2007) (b) Ogunmokun, Ng. (2004) (c) Lages et al. (2004)	(a) Confidence in product price (b) Pricing method, pricing strategy, sales terms (c) Price competitiveness/ value

Source: Extracted from Moghaddam et al., 2011

The services marketing mix model shows that in case of price marketing strategy price competitiveness for a firm is very important aspect and also the firm's pricing strategies play an important role. Promotion marketing strategy includes various promotional and advertising methods used by the firm. Place marketing strategy includes the distribution channel type and network used by firms to export their products. Product marketing strategy refers to the quality and design of the product being exported. It also includes packaging and labelling of the product. The physical environment marketing strategy includes creation and maintenance of physical appearances of the firm's offices established in foreign land. In case of process marketing strategy, the flow of various activities of the firm in the exporting process are taken care of. Lastly, the people marketing strategy includes managing the human side of the enterprise which includes both employees of the firm and customers related to the firm.

According to the literature for product marketing mix important dimensions that emerged include product design, product quality, brand mix and after sales services. One very important dimension of the product marketing mix that was emphasised in literature was product innovation. In case of promotion marketing strategy, the literature indicated important dimensions such as commercial presence of the firm, advertising, trade promotion, sale promotion, personal selling and advertising expenditure. Place marketing strategy includes own centers, exporting channel, dealer network, and direct purchasing as important dimensions suggested by the literature. For price marketing strategy, according to the literature the important dimensions emerged to be confidence in product price, pricing method, pricing strategy and price competitiveness/value.

Literature on export performance has also discussed and considered firm and industry level major issues of (a) managerial; referring to the issues related to decision-makers of the exporting unit, (b) organisational; referring to the characteristics of the exporting unit, (c) environmental; macro influences on the exporting unit, (d) export targeting; referring to segmentation of international markets, and (e) marketing mix or export marketing strategy based on four Ps, namely price, promotion, product and place. The perceptions of managers regarding the major components of the above issues have been presented in Table 2.5.

Table 2.5: Major Managerial Perceptions Regarding Determinants of Export Performance

Total number of respondents (1033)

Perception Variable	Number	Percentage	Category
Product quality	302	29.23	Marketing Mix
Price competitiveness/ value	210	20.32	Marketing Mix
Service quality	67	6.48	Marketing Mix
Competition degree	46	4.45	Environmental
Design	32	3.09	Marketing Mix
Relationship with importers/trust	40	3.87	Marketing Mix
Brand image	29	2.80	Marketing Mix
Distribution network/ availability	24	2.32	Marketing Mix
Innovation	18	1.74	Marketing Mix
Strategy adoption	17	1.64	Marketing Mix
Promotion	15	1.45	Marketing Mix
Product differentiation	19	1.83	Marketing Mix
Foreign market characteristics (dimension/potential)	12	1.16	Export targeting

Source: Extracted from Lages et al., 2005

According to the perceptions of managers of European Union firms, product quality was the most important determinant of export performance with 29.23 per cent votes. Product quality comes under the marketing mix category of the major issues. Price competitiveness/value which again comes under the marketing mix category received 20.32 per cent votes of the managers and was registered as the second most important determinant of export performance. It was followed by service quality with 6.48 per cent votes and belonged to marketing mix category. Degree of competition was voted next by the European Union managers with 4.45 per cent votes and it belonged to the environmental category. Design, relationship with importers, brand image and distribution network received 3.09 per cent, 3.87 per cent, 2.80 per cent and 2.32 per cent votes respectively and all these determinants belonged to marketing mix category. Innovation, strategy adoption, promotion, product differentiation and foreign market characteristics received 1.74 per cent, 1.64 per cent, 1.45 per cent, 1.83 per cent and 1.16 per cent votes respectively. Innovation, strategy adoption, promotion and product differentiation belonged to marketing mix category whereas foreign market characteristics belonged to export targeting category.

Analysis of managerial issues and perceptions affecting the services exports reveals that the services exports marketing mix is the extended version of goods marketing mix and includes three new important approaches towards people, physical presence of the firm and the process followed to deliver services. These three aspects of the services export marketing mix play an important role in services exports and are also considered as the major determinants of services exports. Proper interaction with customers through a well-furnished and well-equipped office and through highly trained staff helps in impressing customers and acts as a catalyst in services exports. The process of delivering services and the after sales services and assistance is also important in new world services exports and these three components should be taken special care by the services exporting firms. The literature also mentions some important dimensions of services marketing mix and these dimensions need special focus by exporting houses in order to improve their exports. Some of these important dimensions include product innovation, after sales services, advertising and trade promotion, pricing strategies and price competitiveness. These days' managers have also their own respective perceptions regarding determinants of export performance. Product quality, service quality, brand image and innovation are a few very important determinants as suggested by managers and their main focus in exports is to take care of these aspects. The overall analysis of determinants of export performance indicate that the most important aspect in modern world trade is to continuously innovate the product and try to create new and different products from your competitors and stay ahead in the race.

2.5 Services Exports of India: Policy Initiatives and Approaches

Foreign trade policy of any country plays an important role in promoting and facilitating foreign trade. The kind of institutional and governmental support needed by firms who deal in foreign trade is provided by the rules and regulations, schemes, subsidies and guidelines incorporated in the foreign trade policy. Foreign trade policy is especially needed in developing and emerging countries since exporters and importers in such countries are not fully experienced and capable of trade all by themselves. In this part of the chapter, Indian Foreign Trade Policy (2009-14) has been discussed and the important schemes and major areas of focus have been talked about. Indian foreign trade policy aims to double India's exports of goods and services by 2014 and in order to achieve this objective the foreign trade policy of India has introduced special focus initiatives in the areas like market diversification, technological upgradation, support to status holders, agriculture, handlooms, handicrafts, gems and ornaments, leather, marine, electronics and IT hardware manufacturing industries, green products, exports of products from North-East, sports goods and toys sector (GoI, 2009). Indian foreign trade policy also includes sectoral specific strategies in order to boost trade in those sectors in which India has potential but yet are to tap that potential. Not only the focus of foreign policy is to encourage foreign trade but its domestic focus is to develop and support certain regions of the country like North-East and J&K by specific policy initiatives provide specific promotional schemes for this purpose.

In the Indian foreign policy of 2009-14 stress has been laid on market diversification and technological upgradation. After the crisis of 2008-09 government was forced to think and formulate a way to sustain and insulate Indian exports from the decline in exports demand from developed countries. So in the foreign policy of 2009-14 new policies were introduced which encouraged diversification of Indian exports to other parts of the world which included countries of Latin America, Africa and Asia. India needs to upgrade and move up in the value chain of exports and there is an urgent need for India to upgrade its technological infrastructure to support its exports. Services sector needs special packages and dedicated policy focus to improve as modern services exports need a strong technological, communication and IT backbone in order to export international standard services from India (GoI, 2005).

Among the other policy initiatives include introduction of new schemes and promotional measures. Some of these are discussed here and first include scheme for Assistance to States for Developing Export Infrastructure and Allied Activities (ASIDE). The motive behind introduction of this scheme is to encourage states by providing them assistance for creating infrastructure which would help in development and growth of exports. Market Access Initiative (MAI) scheme inculcated in the Indian foreign policy helps with financial assistance for export activities with main focus on creating new markets in new countries and also focus on specific and new products which are being exported (Prasad, 2005). Market Development Assistance (MDA) scheme also provides financial assistance, but for promotional activities like trade fairs in India and abroad. Another important scheme introduced in trade policy includes financial help and provides recognition to industrial clusters which are engaged in exporting. It is called Towns of Export Excellence (TEE) and in this scheme government recognises towns which have emerged as exports hub and provide them special status and incentives. There are other types of schemes which ensure quality and standard of products and services that are being exported by India so that

Indian exports are of international standards and would further increase the demand of Indian products in international market. These schemes include Brand Promotion and Quality scheme with main focus on promotion and creating awareness of Indian products in markets overseas. Test houses are being setup by government to assist in modernisation and upgradation of products to meet international standards.

The contribution and potential of service sector in GDP, exports and employment has been significant for Indian economy (Banga, 2005). Therefore, there is a dire need to look into some important policy issues regarding the service sector, especially services exports. Experiences of many countries reveal that a comprehensive policy and strategy positively facilitate the services exports. The basic objectives of the services trade policy of India during the post GATS regime were to ensure that the potential benefits are reaped and threats should be minimized. But services trade has faced many challenges such as consumer protection, service delivery, quality, cost, competition and efficiency and equity tradeoffs. FDI, disinvestment, tariff, credit and finance and other general and service sector-specific policy issues have been indentified and remained the major services trade policy issues in India (Prasad and Sathish, 2010). In the present analysis, the major policy areas such as policy issues for services negotiations, general service policies of India to promote exports, market excess and trade barriers for services, services policy making institutional setup and data issues related to services have been discussed.

The importance of service sector has increased tremendously over the past years and yet the availability of data in this regard is an important issue. The statistics regarding services is very low and this scarcity acts as a hindrance in policy making. Not only the availability of data is an issue but the problem of ambiguity also arises in the available data. There are also some other issues like deficiencies related to service definitions, compulsory standards, regular surveys, classification of data according to some defined and definite pattern, and collection of prices of services for imports as well as exports which need to be taken care of and policy changes need to be done so that the above-mentioned problems related to data deficiency could be solved (GoI, 2001).

The importance of services in Indian GDP has grown and is still growing, but this sector has lagged behind in the aspect of institutional support from the government. There are a variety of services that India exports with their own special characteristics, some services under government control and some privatised and hence the most important need is to setup an institution or a division dedicated for export promotion of services and dealing in all the services. On the lines of goods exports, services exports also need an agency which could provide with relevant information on important areas in services exports to exporters (GoI, 2001). This type of agency or division would cater to all the diversities in the service sector and would act as a medium between Indian exports and foreign clients.

One major policy area that needs special attention is regarding the trade barriers in services sectors and increasing market access of services. Services export faces various visible and invisible trade barriers which limit the market size and hence hamper India's exports. Although due to the GATS negotiations some countries have made commitments in various service sectors to encourage trade and reduce barriers, yet a lot still needs to be done to remove barriers which affects the exports indirectly. Various indirect barriers include standards for quality control, rules and regulations for setting up of offices abroad, visa regulations and such type of rules and regulations indirectly affect the exports of services and commitments should be made by countries in this direction also (World Bank, 2004).

An important issue of policy for services negotiations also needs to be taken care. There is a need to assess the potential of various services and then the future strategies should be formed according to this assessment. There is a need to pursue more focused and more intensive policy approach to promote and increase market access of Indian services in foreign lands (Prasad and Sathish, 2010). The need also arises for more synergy between the growth and development strategies and WTO negotiations. In the future, the negotiations in trade of services need to be realistic and growth and development oriented. India should intensify its efforts to put forward its own agenda before WTO and follow this to fully tap the potential of its service sector.

Promotion of services is a very important part in growth of any service. Recognition of Indian services abroad is essential and the policies of the government should focus on promoting services through various export promotion agencies (Prasad and Sathish, 2010). The policies should also encourage export in various services by helping in financial and legal matters and there is a need to setup Special Economic Zones (SEZs) especially for services exports. Another important step towards services promotion is to encourage free trade agreements or regional trade agreements for services. India's foreign trade policy should reflect dedication and commitment towards promotion and growth of Indian services exports as the services now constitute approximately 60 per cent to the GDP and can play a very important role in overall economic development of India.

Analysis of foreign trade policy of India reveals that it aims at achieving a very ambitious and important goal of doubling exports of goods and services of India by 2014. The policy introduced some new initiatives in some very important fields like diversification of trade and trade markets, technology and electronics and IT. The foreign trade policy also incorporated new schemes and initiatives to encourage those sectors which have untapped potentials and can push Indian exports to a new level. A special focus was given to diversification of trade by promoting a variety of products for exports and opening up of new markets for exports in new countries and expanding Indian export market. In order to provide proper infrastructural support to Indian exports, the foreign trade policy of India emphasised an urgent need to upgrade India's technological infrastructure and create a strong support system for exporting firms. The policy document also introduced a number of promotional schemes to support and help exporting firms to grow and expand market for their products. Some schemes introduced in the trade policy also focused at promoting and creating awareness of Indian products exported by India by organising trade fairs and exhibitions abroad. A very important part covered in the trade policy stressed the need to check, improve and maintain the quality of products being exported and for this purpose some new initiatives were introduced in the trade policy. So, it is safe to say that the foreign trade policy of India helps to create awareness of Indian products and help exporting houses to acquire proper infrastructure for exports and acts as a backbone of Indian exports.

2.6 Services Exports: Trade Agreements and Implications

General Agreement on Tariffs and Trade (GATT), the predecessor of World Trade Organization (WTO), was signed and enacted by only 23 members in 1947 with the objectives to reduce tariffs and trade barriers to facilitate and encourage international trade. GATT provisions and procedures have been extremely doing well and remained operative till 1994 almost for 50 years in managing tariffs and numerous trade barriers across the borders.

India had entered into various trade agreements during the post-WTO and GATS period with the rest of the world, in this part of the chapter an attempt has been made to discuss and analyse briefly some of them (GoI, 2013).

India had signed a number of trade agreements with African countries. Some of them have been discussed here. The first is the trade agreement signed between India and Botswana on 19 January 2001. In the agreement, it was agreed that both the countries shall grant each other the Most Favoured Nation treatment. The agreement provided that both the countries will encourage investment and technological cooperation among themselves. Moreover, the import and export of both goods and services will take place on the basis of contracts specially designed for the two countries at world market prices in accordance with international trade policies.

India signed trade agreement with Liberia on 15 January 1999. According to the trade agreement, each country shall provide the other with Most Favoured Nation treatment in respect of imports and exports of licenses, customs duties and various types of taxes applicable to importation and exportation and also transit of goods. Both the countries agreed to liberalise trade and encourage cooperation among the trading companies of both the countries.

Trade agreement between India and Republic of Mauritius was signed on 10 March 2000. The trade agreement emphasised that both the countries should help each other in setting up of joint ventures in trade and various trade-related sectors with major focus on shipping and transport facilities. The agreement also included that both the countries should work out some kind of technical cooperation programmes in the trading sector and would closely monitor their implementation. The most important part of the agreement was to facilitate and encourage the exchange of information related to trade and trade-related issues and matters.

On 18 April 2002, India and the Kingdom of Swaziland signed a trade agreement which provided both the countries to encourage and support investment in technology and cooperation among the countries to create environment friendly for sustaining international trade activities. The agreement emphasised both the countries to take measures to remove trade barriers and increase bilateral trade in both goods and services.

India and Seychelles signed trade agreement on 18 September 1998. The trade agreement focused on availability of information on trade and trade-related issues and a creating an environment that supports joint participation of companies from both the countries to carry on trade in various fields. The agreement also laid emphasis on cooperation among countries in the areas of information and technology and communication. Reduction in trade tariffs and trade barriers was also covered in the agreement and it was made sure that both the countries complied with all the terms and conditions of the agreement and made sincere efforts to reduce trade tariffs and barriers.

India and United Republic of Tanzania signed trade agreement on 14 January 2000. The trade agreement between the countries emphasised them to create cooperation among themselves across the whole range of trade and trade-related activities. The agreement also provided that both the countries shall provide each other with the Most Favoured Nation treatment with respect to import and export licenses and customs duties. The trade agreement also provided both the countries to encourage and support their firms to organise trade fairs and exhibitions in other country and also actively support and organise firms from other countries to organise and conduct trade fairs and exhibitions in their own country.

On 21 April 2003, India and Zambia signed trade agreement which provided both the countries to permit imports and exports of goods free from customs duties, taxes and other similar levies or charges. The agreement emphasised both the countries to reduce and eliminate various types of trade tariffs that earlier effected the trade relations between the two countries. The agreement also provided the clause in which both the countries could impose safeguards, anti-dumping and countervailing duties in case where it has been established that increased imports of goods from other country are being duped or subsidised causing effect to the domestic industry of the importing country. Even though both the countries have provided each other most favoured nation treatment but in case of any problem related to the above-mentioned issues both the countries could impose the restrictions.

On 2 November 2005, six nations signed a trade agreement to promote economic development through a reliable and continuous process of trade expansion among these six countries. These six countries included Bangladesh, China, India, Laos, Korea and Sri Lanka. These developing countries signed the trade agreement to further improve international economic cooperation through the adoption of mutually beneficial trade liberalisation measures. The agreement signed between the six countries included other provisions such as arrangements on lowering tariffs, border charges and fees on import and export of goods and other non-tariff measures to ensure fare and restriction free trade among the member countries.

An agreement on trade, commerce and transit between India and Bhutan was signed on 28 July 2006. The trade agreement encouraged free trade among the countries and also provision of availability of information on trade and trade-related activities on periodic bases to the government agencies. The two countries emphasised on increased commerce activities among themselves and also agreed to take of tariff restrictions and entry problems related to goods imports. The imports of goods originated from third country came under separate rules and regulations and the two countries agreed to impose non-tariff restrictions on entry of such goods. For the two countries increased trade and commerce were the two important points covered in the agreement.

India and Finland signed trade agreement on 26 March 2010. The agreement focused on promoting activities aimed at the development of bilateral economic cooperation. The terms of the agreement provided both the countries to provide support to the business houses and help in developing new business contacts. One of the main objectives of the agreement is also to facilitate the expansion of bilateral trade among two countries and promote economic and investment opportunities in their respective countries. The agreement also emphasised that both the countries should initiative programmes to exchange information regarding economic development, about existing possibilities concerning trade fairs, exhibitions and entrepreneurial missions. The increased cooperation was aimed at creating new opportunities both for the governments and for the firms of the two countries to invest and increase the scope of trade among the two countries.

India and Korea signed trade agreement in 2005. The general objectives of the trade agreement include that both the countries should liberalise and facilitate trade in goods and services and also expand investment among themselves. The trade agreement also included that the countries need to establish a cooperative framework for the purpose of strengthening and enhancing the economic relations of the two countries. The two countries are also supposed to create an environment conducive for more favourable business conditions and promote fair competition in the free trade area. The governments of both the countries are suppose to make a framework of transparent rules and regulations to govern and monitor trade and investment activities taking place between the two countries. The need to explore new areas of economic cooperation is also stressed in the trade agreement and there is need to develop appropriate measures for closer economic partnership among the countries. The last important point covered in the trade agreement included the need to improve the efficiency and competitiveness of the manufacturing sector and that of services sector of both the countries.

India and Bangladesh signed trade agreement on 21 March 2006. The focus of the agreement was cooperation among the countries in the technological aspects and economic aspects of the trade. Both the countries agreed to promote initiatives that focused on technological improvement and help business units to utilise and incorporate these technologies into their business processes. The trade agreement also focused on promotion, facilitation, expansion and diversification of trade between the two countries.

On 27 October 2010, India and Malaysia signed a trade agreement. The trade agreement included trade facilitative provisions and customs cooperation and trade remedies. The trade agreement included provisions to liberalise trade and a special emphasis was given to services trade liberalisation. This services liberalisation provided with a substantial sectoral coverage which included movement of professionals and skilled persons, cross-border supply and telecommunication services so as to strengthen ties in these areas of interest. The agreement emphasised a transparent and competitive investment regime and the other important areas of focus in trade included infrastructure development, creative industries, tourism, SMEs, business facilitation, science and technology and human resource development.

On 17 June 2003, India signed trade agreement with MERCOSUR (Spanish: Mercado Común del Sur) group of countries. This group consists of four countries, namely Argentina, Brazil, Paraguay and Uruguay. The trade agreement emphasised both the parties to encourage exchange of information on tariffs applied by both the parties on imports and exports. Also the exchange of information included areas like market access, tariff and non-tariff measures, technical standards, anti-dumping and countervailing measures, special customs regimes and dispute settlement. The trade agreement also stressed both the parties to undertake promotion activities such as seminars, trade missions, fairs, symposia and exhibitions in order to give firms a platform to expand their trade activities.

India signed trade agreement with Mongolia on 16 September 1996. The trade agreement signed between the two countries provided for free imports and exports of goods and services from each other on the basis of counter trade. Another clause in the agreement emphasised both the countries to exchange visits of delegations, increase participation in fairs and exhibitions and sharing of trade-related information among the two countries. The trade agreement signed by both the countries also encouraged active participation of cottage, small, medium and large-size enterprises in bilateral economic cooperation. Both the countries agreed to adopt new measures in order to strengthen trade ties among the two countries.

On 29 April 2010, the SAARC countries signed SAARC agreement on Trade in Services (SATIS). The SAARC group of countries includes eight countries, namely Afghanistan, Bangladesh, Bhutan, India, Maldives, Nepal, Pakistan and Sri Lanka. The agreement emphasised that the member countries focused to liberalise and encourage trade in services sector among the group. Some special areas or services sectors were identified in this agreement which were agreed by the member countries to give special care and introduce new schemes and policies to encourage trade in these specific areas. These services sector included aircraft repair and maintenance services, computer reservation system services, selling and marketing of air transport services and other services also included any service in any sector expect services supplied in the exercise of government authority. So, this agreement was focused on development of services sector of the member countries and encouraged them to indulge in trade in the services sectors that are mentioned above.

Preferential Trade Agreement between India and Afghanistan was signed on 6 March 2003. This agreement emphasised that both the countries should adopt new techniques and measures for the expansion of their respective domestic markets through economic integration. The trade agreement also stressed that both the countries should try and introduce policy changes to eliminate any and all obstacles to bilateral trade of both the countries. The major focus of the agreement was that both the countries develop harmonious economic relations among themselves and to provide fair conditions of competition for trade. The trade agreement stressed the countries to reduce or eliminate tariffs on movement of goods which tend to disrupt and create problems in free movement of goods and effect the trade relations.

India and Sri Lanka signed a free trade agreement on 28 December 1998. The trade agreement signed by both the countries stressed them to promote their mutual trade relations as well as promote expansion of trade among the countries. The trade agreement also encouraged both the countries to develop harmonious economic relations among themselves and also provide the firms of their countries to promote fair conditions of competition for trade. Removal of trade barriers between the countries was the other important point that was focused and emphasised in the trade agreement. And also both the countries agreed to reduce and eliminate tariffs on movement of goods and encourage free flow of goods in order to enhance better trade relations among the countries.

Preferential trade agreement was signed between India and Chile on 20 January 2005. The trade agreement signed by both the countries included a very important point that was needed to be taken care and this included concessions on tariffs on a range of products being imported and exported by both the countries. This range of products included meat and fish products, chemicals, metal exports, plastic, rubber, leather products, etc. The agreement focused on free flow of various products in order to generate good trade relations and foster good economic ties between the two countries.

BIMSTEC (Bay of Bengal Initiative for Multi-Sectoral Technical and Economic Cooperation) was signed by five countries in June 1997. This agreement was also called Bangladesh, India, Myanmar, Sri Lanka and Thailand Technical and Economic Cooperation. These five countries agreed on a number of areas of cooperation and some of them were trade and investment, technology, energy, transport and communication, tourism, fisheries, agriculture, cultural cooperation, environment and disaster management, public health, people-to-people contact, poverty alleviation and counter-terrorism and transnational crimes. The areas of cooperation included both goods and new and emerging services sectors in the international trade market. The member countries had to fully cooperate and encourage trade in these areas and should work in the direction to reduce and eliminate trade barriers effecting imports and exports in these important areas of cooperation.

An in-depth analysis of trade agreements that India has signed with other countries reveals two very important trends. Firstly, the focus of these trade agreements before 2000 was reduction in trade tariffs and customs and promotion of trade in goods exports and imports. But with the increasing role of services and growth of Indian service sector and increasing contribution of services trade in Indian GDP the focus of trade agreements after 2000 was trade promotion and reduction in tariffs and free flow of services exports and imports. The services trade among the countries is now the major area of negotiations and India and its trading partners and removing and eliminating barriers in services trade. Secondly, India has experienced a shift in the countries with which it had trade agreements and trade relations. Over the years India has been successful in diversifying its market access and creating new markets for its imports and exports. India's earlier trade partners included a few developed countries like UK. But with expansion in trade, especially exports, India started looking for new markets and eventually new trading partners of India include a number of African, Latin American and Asian countries. Indian economy is bigger than most of these countries and hence these countries act as destinations for Indian exports. The study of trade agreements of India also point out that India is helping some developing countries to expand their domestic market and also providing with basic commodities for infrastructural development in these countries. Countries like Afghanistan and some African countries actually get benefited from these trade agreements and relaxed tariffs and custom duties and get a much needed help to expand their economies. So, it can be concluded that India gains a lot from these trade agreements in terms of reduced/eliminated trade tariffs, free flow of products, etc., but the country with which agreement is signed is also highly benefited and hence these trade agreements are a two-way system of providing trade benefits. Analysis and discussion regarding the trade agreements of India with other countries also show that during neoliberal policy regime trade in services has been liberalized and diversified. This policy of trade agreements have resulted in a changing composition and direction of India's services international trade. Therefore, it emerged that increasing number of trade agreements covering more and more services areas have resulted in growing trade in services and would also positively influence the services trade of India with the rest of the world.

To sum up, the trade between countries is carried out due to differences in inputs and outputs which arise due to different economic conditions, political situations and natural resources endowment available in the countries. These factors, along with some other factors like labour availability, capital, skill development, technological advancement, product innovation, export promotion strategy are considered to be the determinants of export performance.

Indian services sector includes a number of service categories, therefore, service sector of India is governed according to a division of services done by Government of India and its jurisdiction is also divided among Central Government, State Government and in some cases under both Centre and State Governments. On the other hand, classification of services is not this well defined and is not same and varies according to sources. The National Industrial Classification according to Indian Government is different from the classification of services provided by UNCTAD under GATS. And some other sources provide different classifications. There is a need to thoroughly discuss the nature and types of services and to create a new universal classification of services so as remove understanding problem and also solve the problem of ambiguity. The National Industrial Classification of 2008 is provided by the Central Statistical Organisation under Ministry of Statistics and Programme Implementation, Government of India. The international services classification has been provided by UNCTAD under GATS and is divided into two parts. The first part has services classified in old manner as traditional services till the year 1999. With emergence of new, modern and non-traditional services, UNCTAD has provided with new classification from the year 2000 and this classification includes both traditional as well as non-traditional service categories.

Services are different from goods and hence in order to supply services to customers different types of modes are followed which are defined by GATS are cross-border trade, consumption abroad, commercial presence and presence of natural persons. These four modes of supply of services help free and easy flow of services to customers.

Managerial aspect related to services emphasises that the export performance of services depend upon seven Ps of the marketing mix and this extended marketing mix used for services provide managers with a clear path and clear aspects of services exports that need to be taken care in order to improve services export performance. There are new emerging dimensions in services trade according to which new strategies are needed and a special focus on product innovations, brand mix, advertising and trade promotion and new pricing strategies for price competitiveness is need of the hour. Managerial perceptions regarding determinants of export performance also suggest the above-mentioned aspects as important along with some other aspects like product quality, service quality, promotion and product differentiation.

Government of India has given a special focus to promotion of service sector in India and also provided a proper institutional support for exports of services. Foreign trade policy of India has introduced new schemes and promotional activities for services exports and new initiatives are adopted in the policy document that further help in fuelling India's services export growth. The initiatives undertaken by Indian Government in the trade policy provide with incentives, information and means to increase services exports from Indian exporting firms. A special care has been taken to improve and monitor the quality of services being exported from India and certain schemes incorporated in the trade policy help in achieving this goal.

Apart from this, there are certain policy issues that India faces and requires urgent attention. Some of these important policy issues include data availability and ambiguity problem, lack of institutional setup to support exports of services, creation of new markets and increasing market access as well as reduction in trade barriers for services, policy issues related to negotiations in services trade and India's general service policies to promote exports. All these policy issues create a hindrance in services trade; therefore, efforts by state are required in order to solve these issues.

In order to increase volume of trade, especially exports, over the years India has signed a number of trade agreements with different countries. These trade agreements have led to reduction in trade barriers, reduced trade tariffs and custom duties along with creation and expansion of new markets. Free flow of products has become possible now and India has successfully diversified its product range along with a diversified destination market. In the new millennium, services has gained more focus and the trade agreements signed by India during this period include special provisions and initiatives to promote services trade among countries.

❐

Chapter 3

Services Exports of India: Perspectives

3.1 Introduction

Due to the dynamic nature of the trade in services, it requires that researchers and practitioners must keep pace of the changes taking place in the service sector. Recently, international trade in services has emerged subject of intense debate and discussion among the stakeholders. It is apprehended that developing and emerging economies could not gain much in the prevailing global scenario because the provisions and agreements regarding trade in services under GATS and WTO have been in favour of developed economies. Further, many studies in the field also questioned the growth of services and increase in their share of GDP, but not in employment and called it the disproportionate growth of services. For instance, Banga (2005) pointed out, firstly that though the growth of service sector in India has been in line with the global trends, yet the entire decline in the share of primary sector in GDP has been picked up by the service sector rather than by manufacturing sector as in the case of East Asian countries. Secondly, there has not been a corresponding rise in the share of services in total employment and these unique characteristics of service sector have created doubts about its sustainability in the long run. According to this view, this is not going to serve the long-term objectives of the economy which can only be realized by increasing the share of manufacturing sector in the GDP.

Export-Led Growth (ELG) theory has been considered as engine of growth not only by the modern economists and subject experts but also by classical economists (Richards, 2001). Many studies related to developing countries examine the ELG approach and conclude that exports act as engine of growth for these economies (Sharma and Dhakal, 1994; Langhammer, 2002 and Teltscher, 2002). Winsted and Patterson (1998) and Javalgi and Martin (2007) analysed the trends and drivers of growth of globalisation of services trade and find that information and telecommunication technologies, globalisation, origin of WTO and GATS and many regional trade blocs as well as increased service intensity of the manufacturing sector have been the major drivers. It has also been pointed out that Indian service providers are lacking in many areas especially quality, standard and timing (Dossani, 2005). In such a situation, it is of paramount importance to explore and investigate the problem so that some new policy measures can be suggested which may be of desired help to the service export fundamentals of the Indian economy. The inter-relationships among growth of exports of goods and services exports and resultantly impact of this on Indian economy especially on economic growth and employment must be the central problem of the present endeavour.

In the development of every new field of study and research, a stage is reached when it becomes indispensable to take stock of the research work carried out in the past. There is a growing volume of literature of varying quality in field of international trade in services. Some of the studies are not easily accessible to individual researcher and even some significant studies have yet to be in the public domain. In the present study, an attempt has been made to review and make re-appraisal of some of the important research work done by different scholars in the area of service exports. This chapter has been organised into six sections and section 3.1 introduces the importance of review and its relevance. The issues and literature on trade in services such as concepts, definitions and provisions and agreements under GATS has been reviewed in section 3.2. The studies related to the composition, direction, production, and competitiveness of trade in services have been dealt in section 3.3 of the chapter.

In section 3.4, the literature dealing and assessing the impact of international trade in services on poverty, economic growth and employment has been discussed. The studies examined the trade in specific services such as IT, telecommunication, health, education and training, etc. have been reviewed in section 3.5. In the final section 3.6, major research gaps have been presented.

3.2 Trade in Services: Concepts, Definitions, GATS Provisions and Agreements

International trade in services has been open for centuries, even in the absence of any agreements in trade in services among the trading partners. Traditionally, according to WTO (2013) service sectors of the economies across the globe have been considered as domestic activities that do not lend themselves to the application of trade policy concepts and instruments. WTO (2013) pointed out that the General Agreement on Trade in Services (GATS) is the first multilateral trade agreement to cover trade in services among the member countries. It is argued that the implementation of GATS provisions in mid-1990s was one of the major achievements of the Uruguay Round of Trade Negotiations, from 1986 to 1993. The study suggests that the contribution of GATS to international trade in services depends upon firstly ensuring increased transparency and predictability of relevant rules and regulations, secondly by providing a common framework of disciplines governing international transactions, and thirdly by promoting progressive liberalisation through successive rounds of negotiations at GATS and WTO forums. GATS define services on the basis of territorial presence of the suppliers and the consumers in four different modes. These modes include firstly, Mode 1 called the cross border mode, in which services are supplied from the territory of one member into the territory of another; secondly, Mode 2 called the consumption abroad mode, in which the services are supplied in the territory of one member to the consumers of another; thirdly, Mode 3 called the commercial presence mode, in which services are supplied through any type of business or professional establishment of one member in the territory of another; and fourthly, Mode 4 called the presence of natural person mode, in which services are supplied by nationals of one member in the territory of another. Under these modes, GATS has classified services into 12 core service sectors which include business services; communication services; construction and related engineering services; distribution services; educational services; environmental services; financial services; health-related and social services; tourism and travel-related services; recreational, cultural and sporting services; transport services; and other services not included elsewhere. The structure of GATS is very complex and yet it provides great flexibility to its members to manage various service sectors according to their national policy with different trading partners.

Adlung and Mattoo (2008) in the study explained the basic structure of the GATS and also explored the scope and coverage of the agreement. Unlike GATT, GATS is a very flexible agreement which allows member countries to pursue trade in services in accordance to their national trade policies. First section of the study defines services and explains four different types of modes of supply by which services can be traded. The next section of the study explains the comprehensive nature of the GATS. GATS not only covers the traditional nature of services in which movement of consumers and other factors of production take place across border, but it also covers non-traditional nature of services in which movement of factors is not essential in order to carry on trade in services. Next part of the study explains that the flexibility in structure of GATS allows its members to accommodate different service sector-related concerns and objectives in their services trade policy. GATS has made it possible for the governments to pursue policy interests in almost all the areas of concern and carry on services trade harmoniously with other countries. Last part of the study gives overview of the various successful negotiations concerning different countries carried out under GATS till date and it also provides with recommendations to facilitate liberalisation of services trade within the developing countries. In order to further accelerate services trade in the world trade, there is an urgent need to liberalise services trade in the developing countries.

Copeland and Mattoo (2008) in the first section of the study defined services and listed various types of services as covered by GATS. Services can be traded in two methods, first method requires physical proximity between the users and the producers and in the second method services can be delivered through electronic mediums and proximity of users and producers is not necessary. Next part of the study explained comparative advantage and gains from trade as the two main factors due to which trade in services is carried out. Differences in factors of production such as natural resources, technology, labour ratios, etc., lead to comparative advantage of the countries which leads to trade among different countries and hence gains from trade. So, these two theories explain the origin of trade. Next part of the study analyzes various governmental policies that directly or indirectly affect international trade in services. The government policies that favour local producers over foreign producers are called non-tariff barriers and are the most common form of barriers in the services trade unlike tariff barriers which are common type of barriers in goods trade. Various types of non-tariff barriers include discriminatory regulations, licensing, and certification requirements, quotas, etc. The last section of the study emphasizes the importance of trade agreements over liberalizing trade unilaterally. Trade agreements help countries to benefit from reciprocity by ensuring gains to all the countries that signed the agreement and also help to avoid conflicts in trade. The rule-based system in trade agreements ensures these benefits and help in trade liberalisation in an effective and acceptable way to the concerning countries.

Chemsripong and Mahmood (2008) examined the Thailand's service liberalisation scorecard in terms of its commitments to liberalise trade in services and argued that the services sector plays an important role in the economic growth and transformation of a country and the growing international trade in services under GATS provides new challenges and opportunities to services industries. They also pointed out that future economic growth and development depends upon the services sector contribution to GDP, employment, and exports and at the same time apprehended that not all the services are trade sensitive and have comparative advantages. Analysis recommended that there is dire need for specialisation and expertise in providing services and to tap dynamic and potential global services markets for the sustainable growth and international trade in services. The identified dynamic services include informatics, digital media, e-business, health sciences, education and training, logistics management services, agriculture and marine services and professional services. The study also observed that these services have a high global demand and concluded that these sector/industry specific growth drivers would be strategic to promote the services exports. Finally, the study acknowledged the importance of domestic, regional, and global trading environment and infrastructure as a prerequisite for the services sector to promote and sustain international trade and also the need to work and coordinate at various levels such as industry, firm, and mode-specific to grasp the nitty-gritty and underpinnings of competitiveness of the services industry.

Fink and Nikomborirak (2007) in their study examined that how services rules of origin determine the extent of benefits that non-members can have from the trade preferences that are negotiated among members. Rules of origin in case of services are different from the goods as the protection in services does not take the form of tariffs but certain non-tariff measures, ranging from quantitative limitations to regulatory restrictions are exercised. Rules of services origin help to reduce discrimination against non-member countries and help them to benefit from improved market access negotiated under an FTA. However, more restrictive rules of origin may have an opposite affect and limit the scope for non-members. So, agreement policies regarding rules of origin play a vital role in trade negotiations. According to the author, there is limited evidence available that suggests a higher overall growth potential for economies with open service markets.

Sidhu and Jindal (2006) trace out the origin of GATS, stakes in global markets of higher education, issues involved in Indian initiative in higher education to take on GATS. Authors pleaded that the provisions of GATS do not bind any member country to open all of its services to foreign competition and countries are free to choose the services from the list to make its commitment. Further, it is also argued that the foreign competitor can be regulated under GATS provisions of making full commitment, commitment with limitations, or no commitment. Analysis suggests that though some members have apprehensions about the GATS provisions and agreements, it is argued that with the joining of more countries in opening up their services sector to international players real gains of liberalisation and globalisation can be reaped. Hence, it is required to have a strong regulatory framework in place to reap the fruits of liberalisation more efficiently. Finally, the study recommended that India and other developing countries must bargain for removing restrictions under service providing modes under GATS.

Scherrer (2005) in the study described various strategies in the education field that allowed it to be seen as a commodity and hence can be traded. The study discussed the provisions in the General Agreement on Trade in Services (GATS), role of GATS procedures and GATS commitments that are already in the process of the commoditification of education. The study stressed that there is a lot of pressure on various countries to ease trade in educational services and liberalise education services. The study emphasised the need for GATS to provide a new political and legal framework for the purpose of deregulation and privatisation of educational services so as to accelerate trade in education services worldwide. GATS can facilitate and provide safe environment for developing countries to carry trade in education services.

Chanda (2003) in the study examined the effect of interference of WTO in social service sectors such as health, education, and environment under GATS and problems faced by various countries regarding the national sovereignty and autonomy in social policy making due to this interference. The study stressed that most of the concerns discussed are the result of misunderstandings and lack of information about the GATS policies and countries should make efforts to address these problems and work together with GATS to remove ambiguities and weaknesses present in the present GATS framework. The urgent need of the hour is to re-explore and re-write new framework of GATS for policy making by the countries to accommodate new, non-traditional services trade. The study concludes that with the emergence of new service sectors such as health, education, etc., governments are facing new problems related to trade and policy in these services and these problems need to be tackled with the combined efforts of GATS and governments.

Anderson (2001) examined the factors that lead to globalisation and the extent of globalisation along with policy implications for Southeast Asian countries. In the past two decades, the trade reforms have been more unilateral or regional, although there has been a great effort from WTO to encourage all the economies to open up to trade and commit to staying open to international trade and investment. Globalisation has been rewarding economies with good economic governance on one hand, and on the other hand it is also raising the cost for economies with poor economic governance. The indicator for the progress of globalisation is the reducing differences in the prices of goods, services, technology, ideas, financial and other capital and labour. The factors that contributed to this progress include fall in transport costs, massive decline in communication and information costs, and reduction in tariff and non-tariff governmental barriers to trade in goods and services. The technological dimension of globalisation is digital and include lowering of long distance communication costs and cost of accessing and processing knowledge and information. The contribution of governments to globalisation has been very important and government decisions to liberalize goods and services trade have further accelerated the process of globalisation. Emergence of various regional trade blocs has lead to deregulalization of trade among economies and encouraged participation of developing countries as well. The GATT/WTO's contribution to globalisation has been enormous, as the worst abuses in trade are avoided due to the rules set up by WTO and there has been enhanced economic welfare and reduced political tension between the nations.

Holmes (1990) in the paper examined the implications that breaking down of barriers to trade in goods between

Australia and New Zealand can have for trade in services. The first Australia-New Zealand Closer Economic Relations Trade Agreement (ANZCERT or CER for short), was only limited to trade in goods and did not involve issues related to trade in services. It was during the late 1980s that the services were recognised and their growing importance in international trade forced CER agreement to include services in the agreement and reduce trade barriers in the transaction of services between the two countries. The issues related to trade in services which were addressed in the agreement included government monopoly of a service, government controls on entry or capacity, prescriptions of qualifications for entry and rules pertaining to domestic content. The services which have enormously benefited from the liberalisation of trade in services between Australia and New Zealand are telecommunication services, broadcasting, aviation and shipping services and movement of individuals across border. The CER agreement has enabled both the countries to deregulate trade in services and reaps benefits from this. The implications for ASEAN from this agreement are to take a unilateral government action and deregulate trade in services so as to expose public providers to international competition and allow free flow of FDI. These measures can be useful to improve the quality and efficiency of services provided and will also help in regulating cost and price increase.

Hirsch (1989) in the study distinguishes between the characteristics of services and goods and draws a framework of these characteristics for both goods and services. The author in the later part of the paper examines the tradability of the services and premium costs associated with services exports and then draw the conclusion. Like goods services are also acquired by consumers to fulfill three functions: instant consumption, enhancement of the user's consumption capacity, and enhancement of the user's productive capacity. The services which fulfill the first function include travel services, entertainment, haircuts, etc., and satisfy the same needs as food and clothing in case of goods. The services in second and third group include health, education, maintenance, training, etc., and these services are human-capital augmentation services. Not only the purpose fulfilled by services is similar to certain goods but the production of both services and goods include same kind of inputs, namely physical capital, raw labour, and skills or human capital. So, the characteristics that distinguishes between goods and services is that the goods are physical objects that can be transferred between economic units whereas, services are defined by the change in the condition of a person. Another characteristic that distinguishes both is that the services are to be considered as flows, whereas goods are considered to be as stocks which can be consumed when the owner feels like. The analytical framework designed in the study incorporated both goods and services. The extension of one framework to both services and goods is possible due to the reason that the input factors for both goods and services are same which include raw labour, skilled labour and physical capital. The intermediate services included in production of goods and production of services may also be same and hence the production process for both remains the same. In the next part of the study, the tradability of services and of service-intensive goods is discussed. When both the producer and the user of the services and service-intensive goods are located in the same country then the cost of services and goods is the lowest. When the producer and user are located in different countries then some more cost elements are incurred. As the distance between the producer and user increases the cost of transportation and communication tend to increase. When transaction takes place in two different currency systems and in more than one legal jurisdiction, the cost of financing rises. These cost elements are same for both goods and services, but there are other costs like cost incurred due to cultural distance of two countries or cost due to language difference which are specific only to service products. This implies that the international transaction of services include cost premium in addition to domestic service transactions. The study summarizes that even though the input factors of both goods and services are same, yet the fact that services are considered as a flow and affect the condition of the user or the good and goods are tangible and can be consumed at will distinguishes between goods and services. The tradability of the services in international market is affected by the premium costs that are incurred due to distance between the producer and the user. With innovation in communication technologies the cost of services has reduced and there is further need to reduce such premium costs so as to increase the tradability of the services.

3.3 Trade in Services: Composition, Direction, Production, and Competitiveness

World Economic Forum (2013) in the report described the performance of advanced emerging, and developing economies. In the recent years, emerging and developing countries have emerged as important drivers of global economic recovery whereas advanced countries are still struggling to keep pace with economic development. Though the countries are recovering from economic slowdown, still challenges for long-term sustainability remain for them. In order to achieve sustainable growth and policy competitiveness, states need policy actions and also need to focus on important factors that underpin national competitiveness. These important factors include institutional setup, efficient infrastructure for functioning of economy, stable macro-economic environment, effective social structure in health and primary education, quality of higher education and training, efficient goods market, flexible and efficient labour pool, strong financial market structure, technological infrastructure, large market size, sophisticated business practices, and the most important factor, innovation. All these factors need to be inter-linked and development of one leads to a positive effect on another. So, all the factors need to grow simultaneously in order to achieve competitiveness and weakness in one factor often has a negative impact on others. Factors such as institutional setup, infrastructural development, stable macro-economic environment and effective health and primary education system act as a key for development in factor-driven economies. Other factors such as quality of higher education and training, efficient goods market, flexible and efficient labour pool, strong financial market structure, sound technological infrastructure and large market size of economies act as a key for development in efficiency-driven economies.

Remaining factors such as sophistication in business processes and innovation act as a key for development in innovation-driven economies. Therefore, the world economies need to strengthen their infrastructure in social, financial and market structures in order to achieve competitiveness.

Banga and Kumar (2010) examined the contribution of India's services sector to economic growth, composition of India's exports of services, implications of global economic crisis on India's exports of services, estimates of global demand for India's services, the sources of total factor productivity growth in IT services and highlight the role played by global demand and productivity growth. The study indicates that during the post-liberalisation era the share of India's services sector in economic growth have been increasing and now it has reached such a position where contribution of both agriculture and manufacturing sector has been reduced considerably. For instance during 2008-09 in the overall growth rate of GDP of 6.7 per cent the contribution of services was 5.9 per cent, 0.5 per cent was of manufacturing and 0.3 per cent that of agriculture. The growth momentum gained by GDP in recent years is the result of growing service sector and the rising standards and demand of Indian services. They have analysed the various services being exported by India and have found that the major contribution in exports of services is of the software services. The other services which show a promising rise are communication and business services. The study highlights that global economic crisis resulted in decline of Indian export of services. But growth of software services has shown remarkable buoyancy to this crisis in comparison to other services. This may be due to the practice of production cost cutting which becomes priority during global slowdown. Further, there has been changing direction of export of services which have resulted in sustaining the exports of India's software services. On the issue of impact of supply side factors, it is found that average annual growth rate in the growth of total factor productivity increased in the first decade of the millennium. For this, technological advancement has been attributed.

Saez and Goswami (2010) in the study examined the performance of developing countries in services trade. Due to technological innovations and improvements in telecommunication infrastructure, non-traditional services can now be easily exported at virtually zero costs. The study lists the various determinants of trade in services, particularly for developing countries. Services which are low in cost and high in quality produce economy wide benefits and play a very important role in the economy. Some services such as financial services, telecommunications, transportation and other services are inputs for the production of goods, and hence are important determinants of economy wide competitiveness. In next part of the study, author examined and found out that many developing countries have created a niche for themselves by exporting certain types of services both within their own regions and to high income countries. Therefore, there are differences in patterns of trade among these developing countries and also the geographic patterns of trade differ, that is, destination markets also differ. In the next part of the study, the author highlights the various determinants of trade in services. The most important determinants discussed in the study include human capital, research and development intensity, market size, trade in goods, the presence of an English-speaking workforce, quality of infrastructure, the openness of the trade policy regime toward the various modes of services delivery, cost of human capital, and common laws/legal systems. In the last part of the study, author advocates the need to create a "knowledge platform" that would bring together developed, emerging and developing countries so that they could learn from each other's experience in trade and formulate their own trade strategies to improve their performance in world trade.

Serin and Givan (2008) in the study examined the comparative advantage and competitiveness of Turkey. The study suggests that Turkey clearly has a comparative advantage in certain products over other countries but its advantage has been declining lately. The emergence of new rivals for Turkey as well as increased members of European Union have further created problems for Turkey's trade and will affect its comparative advantage and its competitiveness. New regulations regarding exports introduced by European Union have also contributed to this decline and states own trade policies are also not aligned with its trade interests. The revealed comparative advantage index applied in the study revealed that in general Turkey had comparative advantage and Turkish fruit juice sector has performed better than fruit juice sector of Greece. Comparative export performance index applied in the study revealed that Turkey had competitive advantage over Greece and Italy in terms of Olive oil exports. The study concluded that Turkey has advantage in trade of certain commodities over its rivals but introduction of new European Union members and trade policies of Turkey and EU have lead to decline of this advantage over the years.

De and Raychaudhuri (2008) examined the composition and competitiveness of exports of services and its impact on income, poverty and growing income inequalities in India. The study pointed out that during last decade trade in services, both exports and imports of services, has tremendously increased. Even though import of services increased, India was still able to maintain its positive trade balance in services and it was also able to increase its contribution in global trade in services as well. While the major services which India exports constituted of non-traditional services like financial services, information and communication technology services. On the other hand, the import basket constitutes of services like construction, insurance services, and transport and travel services. On the issue of competitiveness in trade in services, the reduction in trade barriers in services resulted in high quality of services and thus high degree of competitiveness. The study also suggests that India is losing its advantage in traditional services and gaining comparative advantage in non-traditional and emerging services. India has seen a great and continuous rise in its per capita income which is the result of growth of services exports and increase in trade in services. The study noted that there has been reduction in poverty, both urban and rural over past decades but the income inequality figures have not changed much. Services exports have definitely played important role in reducing poverty in India but still has not shown any positive effect on income inequality. The study concludes that India has shown a promising rise in trade in services especially services exports which resulted in high growth rate, and achieving competitiveness in several services and reduction in poverty, but it still has to work hard to reduce income inequality and obtain overall growth.

Gabriele (2004) in his study examined the main trends in international trade in services over the past few decades, concerning mainly developing and transition countries. According to the author, the data available for international trade in services is limited and there are few shortcomings and methodological problems affecting statistics on international trade in services. The data analysis in the study indicates that the major exporters of services among non-developed countries are either European transition countries or relatively advanced semi-industrialised Asian and Latin American developing countries. The data also indicates that there are some developing countries that have specialized in one or few specific services sub-sectors. The next part of the study examined how services exports have become the most dynamic component of world trade and the world market share of developing countries has been on the rise. In the late 1990s, a generalized deceleration in the expansion of world trade in services occurred, which slowed down the growth rate of services exports from developing countries. In last part of the study, author explained that most of the export-oriented service activities in developing countries are concentrated in traditional services sectors and are very poorly integrated to the rest of the domestic economy. Therefore, the potential of such services as engines for overall growth is relatively weak. To make the situation worse the economic policies pursued by the governments do not encourage the trade in services.

Kapur and Moitra (2001) in their research study had examined the changing business environment of India. Economic liberalisation of India have created encouraging market conditions for investors and have opened new doors for young entrepreneurs to easily exploit the opportunities available and gain competitive advantage in knowledge-based services. The study emphasised that the success of software services in

India has given hope to other knowledge-based services in India to grow and compete in international markets and replicate the success achieved by Indian software services. Further, on the issue of competitiveness that India has achieved, skill-intensive and tradable services have earned an edge and created a distinction in the world. Unlike other emerging economies of the world, India has shown great progress in services like software, IT, biotechnology, pharmaceuticals, healthcare, etc., which are all knowledge-intensive services and require human-skills. Authors have analysed and concluded that the success of software services and software exports have a spill over affect on other services exports as other services are also showing promising growth and the contribution of all the services exports have fuelled the growth of Indian economy. Increase in service exports of India have not only given momentum to economic growth in the country but also contributed substantially in international trade. After the liberalisation of trade, India has attracted a huge amount of FDI especially in service sector. India has become a favoured destination of FDI inflow and also collaborations with foreign firms have helped Indian firms to grow and mature and create a reputation of their own in the international market. They examined that the progress shown by India is difficult to be replicated by its counterparts as the stimulating and supporting factors like cheap and large skilled labour pool, English-speaking capability, institutional and legal setup are not available with them. The colonial past of India has worked in its favour and the back-end support required for any industry to grow and progress can nowhere else be found. They have also discussed other emerging services and the joint investments with foreign firms taking place in these services like pharmaceutical, healthcare and educational services are also progressing and attracting huge foreign investments. India is becoming hub for setting up of Research and Development centres by top multinational firms and new Special Economic Zones (SEZs) are being set up to support the growth of these services. Finally, it is concluded that the success of Indian software sector have changed the business environment in India. As a result the firms are now taking more risks and are growing internationally, bureaucracy has taken back seat and

Indian youth is more than ever encouraged to become successful entrepreneurs and compete internationally and help in economic growth as well as social growth of India. At this stage India is confident and is ready to change its traditional ways and emerge as the knowledge hub of the world.

Raipuria (2001) in his study examines the position of India in world services exports and the role played by information and communication in expansion of non-software-based services. The study highlights the growing share of services exports in India's overall exports and on the contrary declining share of services exports in total exports of other emerging countries. The share of exports of services in total exports of developed countries is also less than that of India and is declining. The share of services in total exports is rising in India and also the overall share of India in international trade is rising and it still has a long way to go. The study also analysed and concluded that non-software services like financial services, technology transfers, business services, cultural and entertainment services are expanding at a fast rate with information and communication acting as catalysts. Contemporary methods of business such as e-commerce have helped in growth of non-traditional services exports like legal, accounting, consultancy, education and health. There is an increasing demand of such services and India is taking advantage of this opportunity as a result its exports in these services have been growing at a fast rate. The study concludes that there are many factors which are supporting Indian services exports. A huge pool of skilled labour with technical knowledge and ability to speak English is one such factor. Thus, it can be said that India has achieved competitiveness in exports of services which are knowledge intensive and the backbone of this success is its knowledge pool.

Polese and Verreault (1989) in their study attempt to explore and understand the factors which help a particular region to develop and sustain its exports advantages in information-intensive services. In their research, the authors examined how Canada has become a successful exporter of engineering consulting services and how the Quebec region of the country has gained comparative advantage in trade in services. The role of technology, work experience, R&D, external economies, and public policy has been examined in the study. The growth of trade in information-intensive services is a direct result of fall in cost of transportation of services. Services are transported with the help of communication technology and improvements in communication have helped in increasing services trade. Reduction in transportation cost around the world has resulted in more number of persons moving for consulting services which also contributes to increase in services trade. The authors also try to distinguish between the trade in factors and trade in services and transfer of technique and transfer of technology. In information-intensive services when a technique is transferred it does not imply that the underlying technology is also being transferred and hence the export advantage still remains with the exporter and its sustainability is possible. According to authors, in consulting sector the main factors contributing towards competitive advantage are the capacity of the firms to advice and propose different solutions for different clients and adopt according to their problem. Thus, the social skills, technical skills, educational knowledge of the employees play a very important role and help to develop competitive advantage even if there is lack of R&D. Another important factor which has attributed in Quebec's export advantage is its geographical characteristics as its location and size have attracted very large engineering projects. Canada's advantage thus lies in a unique combination of an educated labour force and a geography which required specific engineering skills. Thus, according to the authors factors like geography, accumulated knowledge of the local population, work experience, external environment like location of firms in large cities and pressure on private and semi-private sector to sell their services to new markets contributes to development of export advantages in some regions.

3.4 Trade in Services: Impact on Economic Growth, Poverty and Employment

Banga and Goldar (2007) in the study examined the contribution of services in the manufacturing sector as an input in production process. Services act as input in production process or as intermediaries in the manufacturing sector. The contribution of services has been increasing in manufacturing sector and the data analysis indicates that the contribution of services have further increased after the trade reforms were carried out in the 1990s. This has further fueled the economic growth of India with a continuous increasing share of services in GDP. The growing importance of services in manufacturing sector is due to outsourcing of indirect production activities. Due to advances in technology and growing complexity of manufacturing processes, firms are raising the service content of manufactured goods. So, the two main reasons of growth of services in India, as discussed in paper are lowering of tariff and non-tariff barriers and increased use of services as input in manufacturing sector. The study concludes that the importance of services as an input to production in the manufacturing sector increased considerably in the 1990s as compared to the 1980s. The contribution of services to the growth of manufacturing output went up considerably, from 1.0 per cent in the 1980s to about 25 per cent in the 1990s. The trade reforms of 1990s increased the competition in the domestic market and were responsible, to some extent, for the increase in the intensity of use of services in the manufacturing sector. The findings of the paper also suggest that there is a possibility that the Indian service sector might not only succeed in sustaining its own growth but might also help in improving the growth rate of industrial sector in the near future.

Eschenbach and Hoekman (2006) in their study highlight the structural changes that have taken place in the well-planned economies and the differences that still exist across transition economies. These changes and differences are studied with respect to services intensity and services policy reforms. Inward FDI flow is highly co-related with the policy reforms taking place in financial and infrastructure services, including telecommunications, power and transport. As the mobility of individual persons is increasing, so is the tradability of services and in return the share of services in GDP and employment is also increasing. Transition economies have observed a shift in the structure of services since 1990 as the share of services in the GDP and employment have grown rapidly. Trade in services is becoming easier day by day with advances in technology but a commercial presence always remains a requirement to sell services, i.e. FDI. Some of the sectors which have attracted large share of FDI in transition economies are finance, transport, communications, and distribution services. The authors in their study examined the impact of services policy reforms on the services trade and found out that there is a statistically significant positive association between per capita GDP growth and measures of service sector policy reforms. The study established a two-stage "virtuous circle" according to which growth and political reforms foster the efficiency of reforms, which in turn fuels growth. The authors suggested that the services policies in transition countries should be considered important and proper emphases should be given to them in order to increase trade intensity in the services trade and as service sector reforms potentially can do much to enhance economic growth and efficiency.

Banga (2005) examined the critical issues in India's service-led growth and pointed out that service sector has emerged as the largest and fastest-growing sector in the global as well as in Indian economy. India's services sector has witnessed tremendous growth in GDP, but this growth has not been reflected in a corresponding growth in employment, which led to a policy dilemma and doubts have been cast on the sustainability of service-led growth. This has also been strengthened by the rising labour productivity of some faster growing services which further reduced the capacity of increasing employment in this sector and analysis put forward the need to achieve uniformity in the growth of different services as a solution to overcome policy dilemma. The study demonstrates that the absence of any coherent overall policy for services in line with the industrial policy and agricultural policy and carrying the reforms at the sectoral level in an ad-hoc manner have been the probable reasons for lopsided growth in services. It is suggested to undertake some institutional and regulatory reforms at home and international efforts to liberalise trade in services, so that the benefits of higher trade and FDI in services can be maximised.

Banga prescribed some policy initiatives for acquiring full gains of trade liberalisation in services, firstly certain economy-wide efforts should be made to make general environment more conducive to trade and investments in services. Secondly, macro-economic policies like high tariff rates, large fiscal deficits and rigid labour laws may have an adverse effect on competitiveness of services as on goods must be reformed accordingly. Thirdly, the excessive regulations, discretion in the allocation of licenses and permits, corruption and poor quality of infrastructure could adversely affect the growth of services sector. Finally, strong and financially independent regulators should be in place and efforts should be made to improve business environment so that it can go a long way to sustain the dynamism of India's services sector.

Dossani (2005) has analysed the impact of Indian services off-shoring on the economies of the developed world especially the USA. The study discussed definition and classification of trade in services, the pattern of the services outsourced to India, the likelihood of the hollowing out of the middle class in the developed countries and the role of the Indian diaspora in the promotion of off-shore services. The study concluded that during the post-liberalised era among the developing economies of the world only India emerged as a country with large and successful services exports. The study attributed India's success in export of services especially in IT and business processing to the success of private sector entrepreneurship, institution of stock markets, education institutions and other such factors. Further, it perceived the increased threat to developed world if India's success with service export is replicated by other developing countries but at the same time highlighted and pointed out that this cannot happen unless these countries too can encourage entrepreneurship and build strong institutional setup. As far as the pattern of services outsourced to India are concerned the study point out that only some low-end components of services have been moved to cheap production locations where as bulk of high-end components of services still remain with the developed countries. On the issue of hollowing out of the middle class, it put the evidence on record that with moving low-end services jobs from developed countries to emerging economies like India there is an emergence of threat which may lead to hollowing out of middle class from developed countries. Further, it discussed the contribution of the Indian diaspora in the growth of IT and software industry and concluded that though Indian diaspora has played role in bringing investment to India, yet did not make significant dent as compared to their counterparts in China, Hong Kong and Taiwan. Therefore, Indian diaspora should contribute more in bringing foreign investments to the optimal levels.

UNCTAD (2004) in its report attempts to analyse trends in international trade in services, main exporters of services and impact of service exports on economic growth in developing countries. The period 1980-2000 saw a rapid increase in international trade in services exports. The report shows that the growth of exports of services have been on a much faster rate in developing and emerging economies as compared to developed economies during the period 1980-2000. The world trade in exports of services in the new millennium has declined and reached a stage of stagnation with no further rise in levels of exports. The report further analysed and divided the major services exports into various sectors according to the characteristics of the services. This analysis clearly shows that all the major developing and emerging countries of the world are active in international trade of services exports. Further, the study also shows that the exporters of services from the developing countries are quite active and strong in exports of services of traditional services like travel and transport. But with the emergence of new technology and availability of such technology with the developing countries, their exports of services in traditional services declined and exports of services in other non-traditional services like finance, communication started to show new scope and rise.

Gordon and Gupta (2003) analysed the growth and the increasing share of services in GDP of India. They also try to indentify the main services which grew at a great pace in the 1990s and also analysed and understood the main factors behind growth in service sector. On the issue of share of services in growth, the author examines the trend and concludes that the share of services in GDP is growing in India like other developing countries and constitutes the major portion of the GDP as the share of agriculture and manufacturing is declining which is also same as in other countries of the world. The study suggests that the share of services have been increasing in the GDP, but the employment share of services is not growing as it is growing in other countries. India is observing jobless service sector growth and the share of services-employment is very low. The study examines that the increase in income elasticity of domestic as well as foreign consumers, various advancements in technology, use of Internet by common people, boost in telecommunication technology and increasing number of people which use this technology in daily life have enabled growth of several modern services like business services, communication services, financial services, hotels and restaurants, community services and trade services. Some other factors which also contributed to the growth of service sector in the 1990s include various policy reforms and economic reforms which were undertaken by India during this period. The study suggests that if the further deregulation of the Indian service sector continues, there is a great potential and scope of growth of the service sector in India.

Mukhopadhyay (2002) discusses the ever-increasing importance of trade in services, both at national and international levels. In addition to the traditional services being traded nationally and internationally, new and non-traditional forms of services like environmental services, educational and counseling services are also being traded in big way. Due to advances in technology and new and innovative business practices the services which were earlier considered as non-tradable are now being traded easily throughout the world. Further, during the last two decades of the 20 century due to liberalisation and reduction in trade barriers, there has been a huge flow of Foreign Direct Investment (FDI) especially in service sector and the major players who have benefited from the flow of FDI are developing countries. The study also examines that in order to develop Indian economy and to achieve high rate of economic growth; service sector can play a vital role. But for this purpose Indian service sector itself needs to be more mature and should match international standards, in which FDI can play a major role as it can assist in capital inflow, high work standards and spill over of high-end technology.

Kaminski et al. (1996) in the study discussed the reorientation of trade exports of transition economies of Europe and Central Asia. The study focussed that the introduction of liberalisation policies of price and trade by certain countries helped them to increase their trade exports and benefit from new trade policies. It is stressed that the introduction of liberalisation policies alone does not improve trade performance but it requires both stabilisation and liberalisation. It is suggested that liberal rules have little impact on foreign trade and hence focus should be on relaxing export rules as well as domestic prices in case of transition economies. For the medium-run the policy of the state need to focus on both domestic and foreign trade simultaneously and for the long-run an open import regime, privatisation along with liberal exchange rates is a must. At the end the study concludes that the export performance is the indicator of progress rather than objective of transition and both macro-economic stabilisation and price liberalisation along with removal of export controls leads to overall development of the economy in the long run.

Francois and Reinert (1996) in their study explore the role of services in the structure of production and trade and explain some stylized facts after a thorough analysis of data from various countries. The share of services in the employment and GDP of OECD countries has increased and accounts almost 70 per cent in the total share of trade. Modernisation of economies lead to growth in income, this resulted in increased demand of services and hence growth of services sector. Another reason which leads to growth in services sector was the relationship between the services sector and the manufacturing sector. Due to introduction of new technologies in manufacturing sector, on one hand the need of intermediate or producer services increased and on the other hand there was a shift in the employment trend towards the services sector which further accelerated the growth of service sector. The next part of the study critically examines the role of services in the structure of production and covers four main points. First is the employment, the analysis shows that the rise in the employment in services sector is directly linked to the parallel shift towards service activities within the manufacturing sector as there is an increased use of services as inputs in the manufacturing sector. Second, the demand for producer services or intermediate services has fueled service sector growth of OECD countries. The analysis indicates that as the per capita income level rises, value added in commercial services relative to value added in manufacturing also rises and intermediate demand for commercial services relative to intermediate demand for manufacturing also rises. Third, inter-industry linkages explain the shift in preferences from agriculture through manufacturing into services which is due to income elasticity, that means as the income rises the demand shifts from primary sector to secondary sector to tertiary sector. Fourth, only a small share of services sector growth is explained by allocation of non-production activities between manufacturing and services industry, the major factor for increase of growth in services sector is due to change in structure of production. Outsourcing of some indirect production activities from manufacturing sector to services sector is only a small part of overall growth in producer services. The last part of the study explains the economic structure of the OECD economies and the data analysis suggests that the net composition of the exports of OECD countries is in tangible exports whereas; the economies are concentrated in services. The study indicated that the services have a major share in intermediate structure of production and the significance of the services in overall exports is greater as compared to that suggested in direct trade balance.

Damesick (1986) in the paper studies the shift of employment towards the services sector in Britain, role of producer services in growth and regional development. According to the study, the shift of employment towards services sector in Britain is due to the reason that there has been decline in the employment in manufacturing sector and there are very poor prospects of future growth in this sector. The decline of employment in the manufacturing sector is the result of new technologies and innovations in the manufacturing sector which have created labour-saving processes rather than creating new products and new markets. The other reason that explains the growing share of services in total employment is that as the income of the household increases, the expenditure incurred on services increases as compared to expenditure incurred on goods. There have been an increase in specialisation and division of labour within and between the firms which lead to growth of demand for intermediate services, thus further accelerating demand of services. The various service sectors which experienced growth in employment in the country include hotels and catering, civil aviation, medical services, education and public administration. Next part of the study divides the services into three groups which contributed towards overall growth of the employment in the service sector during the period 1971-84. The first group includes services like hotels and catering which come under recreation and leisure services that experienced growth during study period and employment in these services increased drastically. The second group comprises public services in which educational services were the fastest to grow and also accelerated employment growth in the sector. The third group includes all the private services which are considered as intermediate services rather than consumer services. The growth of employment in some other services like financial, business, and professional services is explained by the fact that due to changing input requirements of the manufacturing sector which resulted in need of non-traditional services. But the change in the manufacturing sector only explains a part of the change in employment direction as it is not the only reason for the shift in employment trend. The study concludes that there is no doubt about the fact that employment in services sector has increased rapidly, but there has been an uneven growth of services industries in terms of number of jobs provided and also in the quality of employment provided. Also, there is a need to study the qualitative aspects of the services work as there are not enough substitutes provided for those lost in manufacturing industries. Another aspect that needs to be examined is the skills of the workers previously employed in manufacturing sector does not necessarily match the skills required in the services sector, therefore, making it difficult for transition to take place.

Spero (1983) in the study examines how services have emerged as a dominant force in the developed countries and a structural change has occurred by transition from agricultural to manufacturing and now to services-based economies. The member countries of General Agreement on Trade and Tariffs (GATT) have acknowledged the changing pattern of international trade and efforts have started to broaden the scope of international trade regime. Further, the study examined that with the economic transactions of other industries the demand for intermediate services or producer services have increased hence, demand for services like finance, insurance, law, advertising, consulting and data processing increased. This shows a shift in the demand pattern of the services as earlier only traditional services like hotels, restaurants, etc., were in demand in the market. Rise of service industry is no doubt a global phenomenon, but the greatest expansion of service sector has taken place in US, as US is the largest exporter of services, followed by Japan. Next part of the study examines how services operated in politically sensitive economic sectors have been highly regulated and government control over communications, banking, insurance, etc. discriminate against foreign service providers. The restrictions can be in form of licensing procedures, discriminatory taxation and denial of the ability to establish branches or subsidiaries and are known as non-tariff barriers. To remove the barriers in services trade and regulate the international trade in services, efforts are in progress to cover trade in services under international trading rules. At the end, the study suggests the need to regulate and systematise trade in services and advocate equal opportunities for developing countries so as to encourage their participation in international trade. A proper set of rules and principles is needed to remove non-tariff barriers and encourage participation of all countries.

3.5 Trade in Services: Specific Services

Woodward (2005) examined the trade in health services and discussed that the health services are not seen for trade benefits but rather its potential effects on health care system are stressed. In most of the developing countries, health services are yet to be considered as a form of trade and hence its importance in services exports is still to be debated. The domestic regulations present in the health sector of various developing countries restrict trade in healthcare services and hence trade-related benefits are yet to be reaped by various countries. The first part of the study discussed the GATS applications in the health services and the set of rules relating to policies that effect trade in these services. The presence of rules for governments in the trade of health services, in this sense, act as restrictions to the trade unlike other provisions in GATS which encourage trade in various service categories. The next part of the study discussed the trade-related benefits of health services and how can governments provide better healthcare facilities for welfare gains and simultaneously it can increase its trade in health services and earn economic gains. Further, it is discussed that exports of health services leads to generation of much needed foreign exchange, rise in employment and income of the countries. In the last part of the study, the author states that the present fundamental principles of the GATS are inappropriate in the health services as they focus mostly on trade-related issues and neglect the basic objective of overall development of health systems to raise the standards of living.

Cowhey and Klimenko (2004) in their study examine the tele-communications market and track its progress over the years and list the challenges that the industry still face. The study also discusses how developments taking place in tele-communication sector in a particular country can be embedded in the international trade and world market. Global tele-communications services market experienced a revolutionary change in the 1990s as the digital technology was being introduced in the industry which led to increase in number of private firms acquiring this technology and entering the market which changed the monopoly system and as a result competitive entry and market pricing of services came into picture. In order to exploit this opportunity, major developed countries wanted to target developing markets and were impatient to make commitments on liberalisation of completion and trade in telecom services with developing countries. So, the WTO agreement on liberalisation of markets and regulation of trade in telecom services was adopted and signed by 67 countries making binding offers on market access. The agreement drastically changed the international tele-communications regime and had three major implications. First, there should be a significant minimum commitment from the countries which are still not the members of WTO and the agreement has set the terms of their accession; second, as the traditional tele-communication practices are believed to be less sustainable so the demand for regulatory transparency is more and the countries with less transparency are considered to be risky; and third, demand of introduction of new technology and products in the services has increased and also there is reduction in the prices of cross-border network services. The next part of the study explains some basic principles which will affect the future of tele-communication market policies. In order to prevent natural monopoly in the market and maintain competitive structure the tele-communications industry needs to follow special cost characteristics so as to maintain rate balance in the market. Operating cost for tele-communication services decreases with high density areas; therefore, demographic landscape is an important factor for tele-communications infrastructure deployment. The policies also make it mandatory for old firms to share network with new entrants so that there are less barriers to entry. On the issue of credibility of regulatory systems in various countries, the study states that the regulators have made it sure that there is no attempt by big and influential firms to practice undue market power and it has been made sure that the services are supplied at minimum cost. As the implication of this OECD countries were able to invest in expansion and modernisation of their tele-communication industry. In the last part of the study, the authors have listed the challenges that the tele-communication services sector still faces. According to them, there are three major policy challenges that need focus. First is the important and critical role of rate rebalancing, as all the countries are facing the problem of escalated prices for international services and these inflated communication and data services hinder creation of an information-based economy. Second challenge is the challenge of getting interconnection policy right for international telecom services. The study suggests introduction of some international benchmarks so that the interconnection costs can be easily regulated. Third, the challenge of setting up a credible regulatory process so that the dominant players do not misuse their powers and there is equal opportunity for every firm to compete in the international telecommunication market.

Daniels (2002) in the study examined that with the increasing tradability of 'basic' services like transportation, insurance, etc. there has been a rise in the international profile of services. The study stressed that the contribution of indirect services to the international trade should also be recognised and further encouraged since the contribution is substantial. In terms of regulation and information, some countries are better and more advanced than others and can better capitalize on global developments in service trade and FDI. Services play a dual role of facilitator and a product of economic growth and development due to their dynamic synergy with the manufacturing. Further, the study states various drivers which lead to growth of services trade. These drivers include increased efficiency of information and communications technology networks, deregulation of many services such as telecommunications, financial services, in national markets and harmonisation of cross-border transactions or human mobility within trade blocs, and equal treatment of national and foreign service providers. Even though the share of services has increased in world trade, then also there has been no sign of a dramatic shift towards services in world trade at the aggregate level.

Fink et al. (2002) in the present study examined the two important reasons for high maritime transport costs in some countries, which include restrictive trade policies and private anti-competitive practices. The authors argue that the trade liberalisation in case of maritime transport would lead to an average of one-third of lower linear transport prices along with huge cost savings. Further, the study states that the cargo reservation policies do not act as a barrier to trade anymore. The study suggests that there is a need to eliminate various policy restrictions to trade in maritime transport services in order to increase the gains. Apart from policy restrictions, private anti-competitive practices of international maritime cartels also need to be addressed. There is need to create sector-specific competition rules and also there is a need to strengthen the general GATS disciplines. These measures if implemented fully would help in regularising transport costs and would protect the market access rights of foreign supplies. In designing and implementing such competitive rules, the main problem would be faced by small countries as large states have the power to negotiate and strictly enforce such laws but small states cannot. And lastly the study stressed the urgent need for various developing countries to come together and jointly commit towards the liberalisation of maritime transport services in order to strengthen their position in international trade market.

Deodhar (2002) explores the possibility of trade in educational services and how India can expand its share of trade in educational services. The General Agreement on Trade in Services (GATS) is an agreement which encourages and regulates trade in commercial services which vary from tourism to consultancy to educational services. The study identifies various issues related to trade of educational services in India and suggest various steps to strategically manage trade in educational services and make commitments in WTO which will increase India's opportunities in trade of educational services. There is a great potential for growth of trade in educational services and government can significantly contribute as most of the leading educational institutions are funded by government. There is a direct competition from private institutes to government institutes; therefore, the necessity of the hour is investment in education and knowledge which are an integral factor of growth for any country. India's GDP growth in the post-liberalisation period has been considerably high and this growth rate is fuelled by increase in total factor productivity which is due to improvement in physical and human capital and access to knowledge. Further, the author has classified the trade of educational services in a two-way classification and tries to explore in which category India can make its presence felt. According to WTO, trade in educational services is classified into primary education, secondary education, high education, adult education and other education. Now the question is that whether it is mandatory for every member country to open all the educational categories? The answer is no. Depending upon the need of the member country some specific categories can be opened up. As developed countries already have a very good secondary and higher education system, they can give more emphasis to adult and other education categories. There is also a second classification which is based on the nature of trade in services, in this case educational services. These modes of classification include cross-border supply mode (includes courses through distance education, online courses, educational testing services, and educational material that is provided overseas); consumption abroad mode (refers to import of educational services through movement of the consumers/students to other country for pursuing education); commercial presence mode (refers to actual presence of an educational service provider of a country in another country); and movement of natural persons (it involves people moving between countries to provide educational services). Next part of the study examines the competitiveness of Indian educational services and suggests some strategies to reform Indian educational system in order to boost trade in educational services. Educational testing services are not new to India and there are some good quality all-India qualifying tests in a selected few fields like management and engineering. Same model can be adopted for various other fields by upgrading basic requirements of computerisation and use of Internet facilities along with actively sorting out markets for such services. Presence of Indian students on foreign campuses is increasing every year and a large portion of these students include post-graduate students in US, Europe, and Australia. The other aspect of this is export of such services, that is foreign students studying in Indian institutions and the present situation is not too good. There are large numbers of students from developing countries which come to India, but very few students from developed countries see India as an option, this is due to the fact that the infrastructure of Indian campuses is poor and not up to international quality. Therefore, there is a need to upgrade the facilities on campuses and attract students from developed countries as well. Establishment of Indian schools abroad is also a very good option for India as till now there are very few CBSE-based schools abroad. The parts of the world where Indian population is considerable can be targeted as there would be great demand for such schools. Export of educational services in the form of movement of natural persons is also an area in which India has potential and there are already a number of teachers and researchers from India who are working in foreign institutions. There is a demand of Indian teachers especially in mathematics, science and English and this trend will also encourage individuals to join the profession domestically as well. The study proposes some strategies for India to increase its educational services exports and emphases on upgradation and improvement of educational infrastructure so that India can compete with developed countries in the global market. Encouraging educational testing services, setting up niche markets in India for specific knowledge programmes, liberalising movement of natural persons, and most importantly upgrading and improvement of infrastructure are some of the urgent steps that need to be taken to encourage trade in exports of educational services.

Kumar (2001) in the study examined the problems of scarcity of talent, rising wage costs and emerging competition faced by the Indian software industry. In the first part of the study the strengths and capabilities of Indian software industry are discussed. Indian software industry has covered a huge distance from delivering low-skilled exports to high-skilled services exports and completing turnkey projects for large companies. The growth of medium and large companies in the Indian software industry has expanded the supply base and hence further accelerated the growth. Increasing professionalism and recognition of Indian software industry on global platform is also a very important reason for the growth of software industry as it aligns Indian software companies to the best global practices. The next section of the study examined the development implications of Indian software industry. Increased growth of Indian software industry has directly impacted the national income and growth of GDP of the country. It has also led to much needed increase in foreign exchange earnings and presently India is one of the leading exporters of software services to the developed countries. Indirect benefits of growth of software services include growth in domestic entrepreneurship, improvement in India's relations with trading partners and change in perception about India in the world market. In the last section of the study, the author has discussed various challenges faced by Indian software industry in strengthening its position further. The major challenges include eroding of labour cost advantages as the salaries and incentives provided in the software industry are increasing. The scarce availability of quality-trained manpower in the software industry is another problem that India faces. India is facing competition from other countries of the world which are fast making progress in software industry. The last challenge India faces is its very little investment in R&D. India needs to pump its funds to R&D so as to raise its standard and climb up the ladder and start exporting software services which require high skills.

Joseph and Harilal (2001) in their study track performance of Indian software exports, the implications of services growth on the availability of skilled manpower and the possible threats that software exports can face. Growth in information and communication technology can have implications on all the spheres of human life and with the diffusion of IT into various parts of society can lead to enormous opportunity of growth in all spheres of human activity. According to the study, the role of state in growth of Indian IT sector have been only as a promoter of IT industry for foreign exchange earnings rather than a facilitator. Till 1980s there were no separate measures adopted to develop software industry and only when the software was recognised as completely different industry policies were formed to further develop this industry. Next part of the study explains the structure of Indian IT exports as trade in software is carried out by three ways: on-site services, offshore services and offshore products and packages. In case of on-site services, exports of manpower take place and development of the software is done on-site. In the offshore services the software is developed in the domestic country and then exported to the users. In offshore packages or software product development neither the receiver nor the producer moves. India's comparative advantage is in offshore services as its share is increasing and Indian software industry competes on cost advantage with very negligible innovations. Implications of IT export boom can be negative as well. In theory, the boom in software export sector would automatically lead to demand for labour in this sector, which increases wage rates and as a result labour from other sector shift to software sector. So, other sectors are forced to increase wage rates as well but in order to curb their expenses they reduce their employment, hence leading to reduction in output. Other affects can be reduction in employment as well as production in manufacturing sector due to boom in software exports. The decrease in IT hardware industry and communication equipment industry is attributed to faulty policies, as the labour market linkages between the hardware and software industry have been overlooked. The last part of the study suggests that in order to sustain growth in Indian software sector the supply of technically skilled manpower must be maintained. As there is high demand of Indian software engineers in foreign, India is experiencing brain drain and the top layer of professionals is moving to other parts of the world. India is thus left with the second best option of skilled manpower which would compromise quality. So, in order to hire best quality professional, higher number of skilled manpower is needed which can work in domestic software industry and also the wage rates should be rebalanced according to international market so that domestic software industry would not face shortage of manpower.

3.6 Research Gaps

The perspectives of literature on international trade in services, regulations and provisions under GATS, composition, direction, competitiveness and exports of different types of services confirms that most of the research has analysed and covered individual services and their role and impact on Indian economy and world economy. Majority of them concentrated on GATS provisions, agreements, future negotiations, role in economic growth, GDP, and employment generation and IT, software and Business Process Outsourcing (BPO) services. Few studies explore the reciprocal inter-relations among services exports, economic growth, and comparative advantage of nation and employment issues exhaustively and comprehensively. Modernization of economies have lead to growth in income, which resulted in increased demand of services and hence growth of services sector. Further, due to introduction of new technologies in manufacturing sector, on one hand the need of intermediate or producer services increased and on the other hand there was a shift in the employment trend towards the services sector which further accelerated the growth of service sector. Some studies examine the factors that lead to increase of employment in services sector and investigate the relation between decreased productivity and employment in manufacturing sector and relative increase in productivity and employment of the services sector.

There are few studies that explore the distinguishing characteristics of goods and services and cover the modes of transaction in services exports. Factors like geography, accumulated knowledge of the local population, work experience, external environment like location of firms in large cities and pressure on private and semi-private sector to sell their services to new markets contributes to development of export advantages in some regions. Further, it is evidently clear that there seems a paucity of studies on exports of services at aggregate level, i.e. analysing the trends and impact of exports of services on economic growth and employment scenario of Indian economy. Therefore, the need for a comprehensive and coherent research arises to conduct on India's exports of services. The present study would be an attempt to fill this gap and aims to study and investigate the role, importance and various other dimensions of the exports of services of India and their impact on Indian economy by including all the exports of services in its scope.

❐

Chapter 4

India's International Trade in Services: Growth and Trends

4.1 Introduction

International trade is the exchange of goods and services between countries and it gives consumers and countries the opportunity to be exposed to goods and services that are not locally available. International trade also allows developed countries to use their resources efficiently and according to theories of international trade, these countries gain from the comparative advantage in production and specialisation. In international trade theory, there are two major reasons for trade between countries, firstly, comparative advantage in cost of production due to differences in technology, natural resources, production function, policies, institutions and other factors. Secondly, gains from specialisation arising from increasing returns to scale or agglomeration effects (Copeland and Mattoo, 2008). The need of international trade arises because the countries have different production capabilities and specialisations in producing different goods and services. The basic and fundamental principle of international trade should be that a country buys goods and services from the country which has the lowest prices and sell goods and services to the country which offers highest prices. Further, international trade has exerted a profound influence on the economic growth across the countries and it is also established that the countries which opened up their economies and liberalised trade restrictions have grown faster over the years (Vijayasri, 2013). But many countries of the world reluctantly opened their economies to protect their people from harmful effects of international trade by introducing barriers and restrictions. To grow faster, sometimes policy-makers in developing countries compromise with the welfare of the people, unwanted dependence on foreign countries, deceleration of domestic industry and loss of jobs (Kuźnar, 2007).

International trade injects global competition and hence domestic industry tends to become competitive and efficient, therefore, international trade is very important and crucial for all the countries in the world. Recently, the issues of international trade and economic growth have gained substantial importance with the introduction of trade liberalisation policies. As a result of this, the volume of international trade (both goods and services) has increased from US $ 6,338,858 billion in 1995 to US $ 22,662,355 billion in 2012 (Table 4.1). Empirical analysis of international trade has clearly established that international trade leads to economic growth provided the policy initiatives and infrastructure are accommodative to cope with the social, economic and financial changes at international level (Nandi and Biswas, 1997). In this chapter, an attempt has been made to study different aspects of India's international trade in goods and services such as overview of world trade, share and volume of goods and services in trade, composition of international trade, direction and growth of India's international trade. To investigate the growth trends of different aspects of services exports following trend growth rate equation/method has been used.

Trend Growth Rate:

Let the equation be—

$$Y = ab^t \quad ...(4.1)$$

Where; Y is the concerned variable

t is the time variable

b = (1 + r); where 'r' is growth rate

'a' and 'b' are constants

taking log on both sides of equation 4.1

$$\log Y = \log a + t \log b \quad ...(4.2)$$

Equation 4.2, a semi-log equation will be estimated by running regression, log y on t, so 'log a' and 'log b' will be estimated.

The trend growth rate 'r' is estimated by taking anti-log of estimated parameter log b, attached to time variable in the semi-log equation and subtracting one from it and multiplying the residual by 100.

4.2 World Trade: Overall Scenario

International trade refers to the trade and commercial relations among the countries. During the last few decades comprehensive development of the international trade has taken place and it is considered to be the most dynamic element of the world economic development. Dynamics of international trade cannot only be observed from quantitative angle, but also from the qualitative and structural changes angle, as presently international trade has been the critical factor influencing the worldwide economic growth. In such a scenario, here an attempt has been made to present the brief overview of the international trade and the information of volume of international trade in goods and services, its growth and annual percentage changes has been shown in Table 4.1 and Figures 4.1, 4.2 and 4.3.

International trade in goods and services has increased from US $ 6,338,858 billion in 1995 to US $ 22,662,355 billion in 2012 with 8.8 per cent trend growth rate during 1995-2012. The international trade in goods alone has registered 8.7 per cent trend growth rate over the same period and value of goods trade increased from US $ 5,116,633 billion in 1995 to US $ 18,196,246 billion in 2012. Similarly, the international trade in services has increased from US $ 1,222,225 billion in 1995 to US $ 4,473,813 billion in 2012 and it grew at 9 per cent over the period. Analysis suggests that the share of goods and services trade in total world trade during post WTO period has almost remained around 80 per cent and 20 per cent respectively with minor fluctuations.

Table 4.1: The Value of International Trade in Goods and Services (Exports), 1995-2012

(US $ Millions at current prices and current exchange rate)

Year	Trade in Goods	Trade in Services	Trade in Goods and Services
1995	5116633 (80.7)	1222225 (19.3)	6338858 (100)
1996	5383163 (80.3)	1317313 (19.7)	6700476 (100)
1997	5590552 (80.3)	1372613 (19.7)	6963165 (100)
1998	5467675 (79.7)	1389978 (20.3)	6857653 (100)
1999	5690630 (79.9)	1435548 (20.1)	7126179 (100)
2000	6418666 (80.8)	1521978 (19.2)	7940643 (100)
2001	6157213 (80.1)	1525108 (19.9)	7682321 (100)
2002	6383936 (79.6)	1634065 (20.4)	8018001 (100)
2003	7456250 (79.7)	1896585 (20.3)	9352836 (100)
2004	9064092 (79.8)	2302354 (20.3)	11365459 (100)
2005	10356477 (80.1)	2573223 (19.9)	12925674 (100)
2006	11980342 (80.5)	2908697 (19.6)	14877488 (100)
2007	13856628 (79.9)	3490237 (20.1)	17336226 (100)
2008	15929433 (80.3)	3916201 (19.7)	19845088 (100)

Year	Trade in Goods	Trade in Services	Trade in Goods and Services
2009	12371247 (77.7)	3555576 (22.3)	15924040 (100)
2010	15077595 (79.5)	3896263 (20.5)	18968720 (100)
2011	18071943 (80.5)	4372893 (19.5)	22438886 (100)
2012	18196246 (80.3)	4473813 (19.7)	22662355 (100)
TGR	8.7	9.0	8.8

Note: 1. Figures in Parenthesis are Percentages, 2. TGR - Trend Growth Rate

Source: UNCTADSTAT, United Nations Conference on Trade and Development Statistics

Analysis of international trade shows that it increased in volume, value and registered satisfactory growth mainly due to liberalisation of trade in goods and services after the implementation of WTO and GATS agreements and provisions.

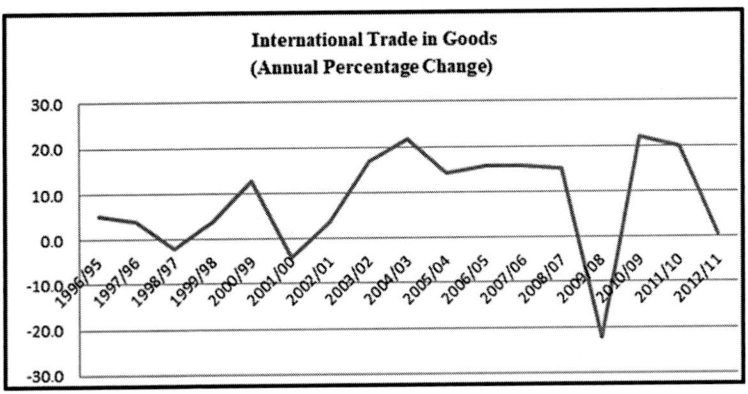

Figure 4.1: Annual Percentage Change in International Trade in Goods, 1995-2012

Source: Based on column 2 of Table 4.1

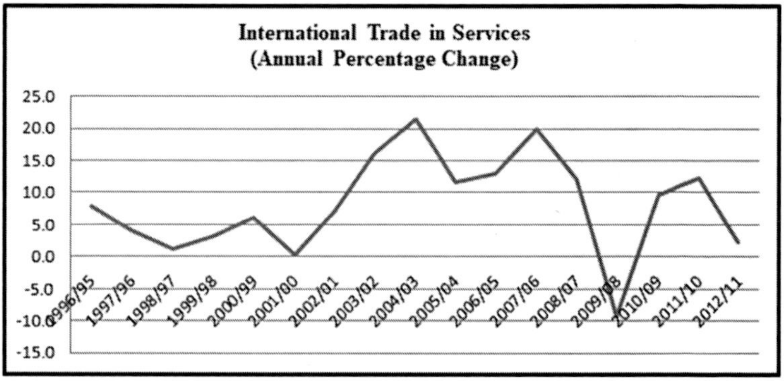

Figure 4.2: Annual Percentage Change in International Trade in Services, 1995-2012

Source: Based on column 3 of Table 4.1

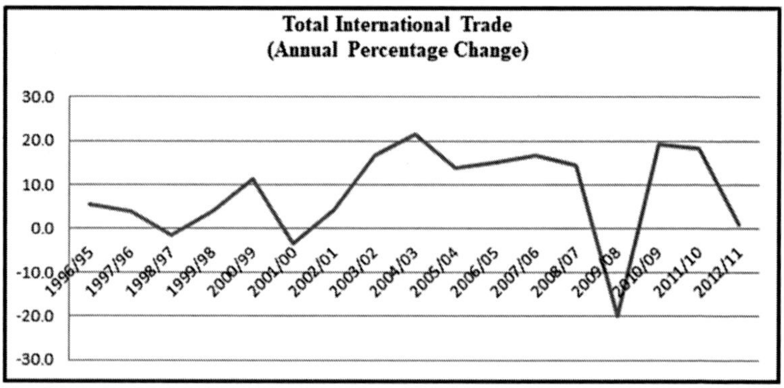

Figure 4.3: Annual Percentage Change in International Trade in Goods and Services, 1995-2012

Source: Based on column 4 of Table 4.1

It can be concluded from the analysis that trade liberalisation has helped the growth of world trade in goods as well as in services across the globe.

4.3 World Trade: Region-wise Analysis

In international trade in goods and services, the major players in terms of their share in world exports were developed countries. However, during previous two decades especially post-WTO period, the share of developing countries has also been increasing in the world trade in goods and services. It is pertinent to mention that it is of paramount importance to look at the shares of various regions of the world in international trade. For the purpose, the WTO has divided the whole world into three broad regions, namely developing economies, transition economies and developed economies (WTO, 2014). In developed economies, USA, Canada, UK, Germany, France, Japan, South Korea and Australia are the major countries. Russia and erstwhile USSR countries are classified as transition economies and China, Brazil, Argentina, India and Malaysia are major developing economies. The information regarding region-wise international trade in goods and services has been depicted in Table 4.2 and Figure 4.4, Figure 4.5 and Figure 4.6.

Analysis of Table 4.2 reveals that world trade in goods has been dominated by the developed countries with about 70 per cent share followed by developing economies with about 28 per cent and transition economies with 2.3 per cent during 1995. However, over the period 1995-2012, the share of developed countries has declined to around 50 per cent of the total world trade in goods and that of developing economies has increased to about 45 per cent and that of transition economies to around 5 per cent during 2012. International trade in goods of developed economies has registered 6.7 per cent trend rate of growth during 1995-2012. But transition and developing economies have witnessed high trend growth rates of 14.5 per cent and 11.9 per cent respectively. Analysis shows that shares and growth of international trade in goods has experienced shifts in favour of developing and transition economies during post-WTO era. It can also be said that direction of international trade in services has changed and now it is more participatory.

Similarly, the total world trade (both goods and services) has also witnessed changes during post-reforms period 1995-2012. The share of developed economies in trade (both goods and services) was around 71 per cent and followed by developing and transition economies with 27 per cent and about 2 per cent respectively during 1995. This position has changed in favour

Table 4.2: Region-wise International Trade in Goods and Services (Exports), 1995-2012

(US $ Millions at current prices and current exchange rate)

Year	Trade in Goods			Trade in Services			Trade in Goods and Services		
	Developing	Transition	Developed	Developing	Transition	Developed	Developing	Transition	Developed
1995	1438977 (28.1)	118032 (2.3)	3559624 (69.6)	273296 (22.7)	–	932449 (77.3)	1712274 (27.0)	134511 (2.1)	4492073 (70.9)
1996	1584225 (29.4)	130138 (2.4)	3668800 (68.2)	293929 (22.3)	22680 (1.7)	1000705 (76.0)	1878154 (28.0)	152818 (2.3)	4669504 (69.7)
1997	1692155 (30.3)	128919 (2.3)	3769477 (67.4)	317158 (23.1)	24234 (1.8)	1031221 (75.1)	2009313 (28.9)	153154 (2.2)	4800698 (68.9)
1998	1560822 (28.5)	112090 (2.1)	3794763 (69.4)	308351 (22.2)	21829 (1.6)	1059798 (76.2)	1869172 (27.3)	133919 (2.0)	4854561 (70.8)
1999	1691870 (29.7)	111932 (2.0)	3886828 (68.3)	319216 (22.2)	18219 (1.3)	1098113 (76.5)	2011087 (28.2)	130150 (1.8)	4984942 (70.0)
2000	2088538 (32.5)	151557 (2.4)	4178572 (65.1)	352035 (23.1)	20190 (1.3)	1149753 (75.5)	2440573 (30.7)	171746 (2.2)	5328325 (67.1)
2001	1955115 (31.5)	150205 (2.4)	4051893 (65.8)	352169 (23.1)	22593 (1.5)	1150346 (75.4)	2307284 (30.0)	172798 (2.2)	5202239 (67.7)
2002	2096811 (32.8)	159499 (2.5)	4127626 (64.7)	378400 (23.2)	26236 (1.6)	1229429 (75.2)	2475211 (30.9)	185736 (2.3)	5357054 (66.8)
2003	2486940 (33.4)	201770 (2.7)	4767540 (63.9)	431953 (22.8)	30763 (1.6)	1433870 (75.6)	2918893 (31.2)	232533 (2.5)	6201410 (66.3)

2004	3145898 (34.7)	275639 (3.0)	5642555 (62.3)	541649 (23.5)	40297 (1.8)	1720408 (74.7)	3687547 (32.4)	315629 (2.8)	7362283 (64.8)
2005	3844419 (37.1)	356271 (3.4)	6155786 (59.4)	630603 (24.5)	47531 (1.8)	1895089 (73.6)	4475022 (34.6)	403473 (3.1)	8047179 (62.3)
2006	4583121 (38.3)	446840 (3.7)	6950380 (58.0)	733859 (25.2)	58960 (2.0)	2115878 (72.7)	5316981 (35.7)	502768 (3.4)	9057739 (60.9)
2007	5361905 (38.7)	540991 (3.9)	7953733 (57.4)	897798 (25.7)	77876 (2.2)	2514563 (72.0)	6259703 (36.1)	614335 (3.5)	10462188 (60.3)
2008	6343766 (39.8)	727824 (4.6)	8857843 (55.6)	1038171 (26.5)	98524 (2.5)	2779506 (71.0)	7381516 (37.2)	826348 (4.2)	11637225 (58.6)
2009	5014944 (40.5)	475153 (3.8)	6881150 (55.6)	929064 (26.1)	83158 (2.3)	2543353 (71.5)	5943676 (37.3)	558311 (3.5)	9422052 (59.2)
2010	6431745 (42.7)	618037 (4.1)	8027814 (53.2)	1109961 (28.5)	90958 (2.3)	2695345 (69.2)	7541493 (39.8)	708995 (3.7)	10718233 (56.5)
2011	7885075 (43.6)	817458 (4.5)	9369410 (51.8)	1252671 (28.6)	108956 (2.5)	3011266 (68.9)	9136751 (40.7)	926414 (4.1)	12375721 (55.2)
2012	8206100 (45.1)	830601 (4.6)	9159545 (50.3)	1353120 (30.2)	117344 (2.6)	3003349 (67.1)	9559220 (42.2)	947945 (4.2)	12155190 (53.6)
TGR	11.9	14.5	6.7	10.9	13.6	8.3	11.7	14.3	7.0

Note: 1. TRG - Trend Growth Rate. 2. Figures in parenthesis are percentages

Source: UNCTADSTAT, United Nations Conference on Trade and Development Statistics

of developing and transition economies during the period 1995-2012, as the share of developed economies in trade (both goods and services) has declined to around 54 per cent and that of the developing and transition economies have increased to about 42 per cent and 4 per cent respectively in 2012. International trade (both goods and services) of developed economies has registered 7 per cent trend growth rate during 1995-2012. But transition and developing economies have witnessed high trend growth rates of 14.3 per cent and 11.7 per cent respectively during the same period. From this, it can be safely concluded that world trade in goods and services has been diverted from the developed world to transition and developing world during post-WTO regime.

However, Table 4.2 also suggests that though origin of trade in services has somewhat changed during 1995-2012, yet not witnessed as sharp diversion as in case of total world trade in goods. The respective shares of the developed, developing and transition economies were 76 per cent, 22.3 per cent and 1.7 per cent in 1996. Over the period 1995-2012 these shares have changed to about 67 per cent, 30 per cent and 3 per cent respectively.

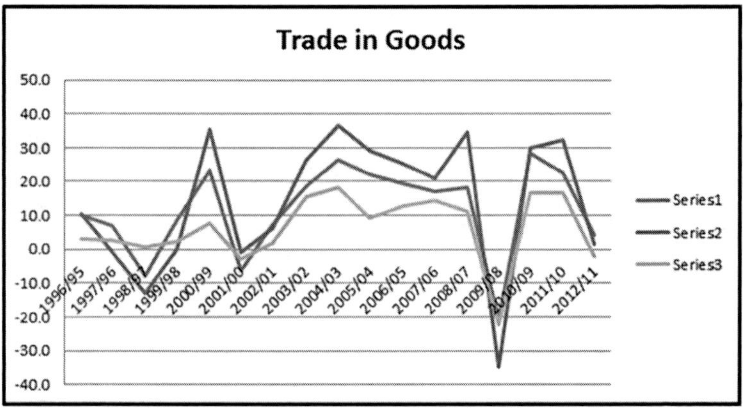

Figure 4.4: Region-wise International Trade in Goods (Exports), 1995-2012

Note: Series 1 - Developing Economies, Series 2 - Transition Economies, Series 3 - Developed Economies

Source: Based on Table 4.2

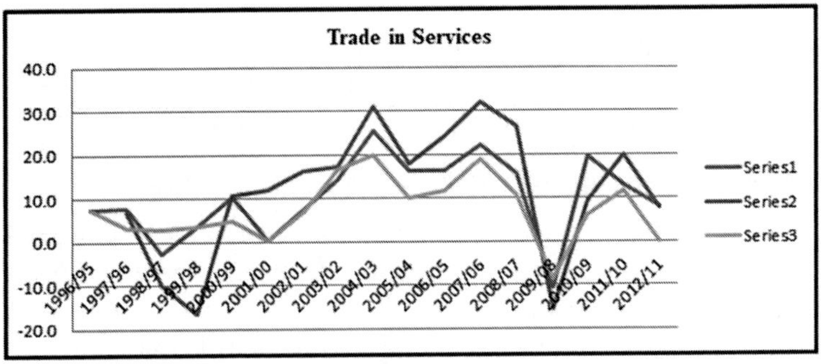

Figure 4.5: Region-wise International Trade in Services (Exports), 1995-2012

Note: Series 1 - Developing Economies Series, 2 - Transition Economies, Series 3 - Developed Economies

Source: Based on Table 4.2

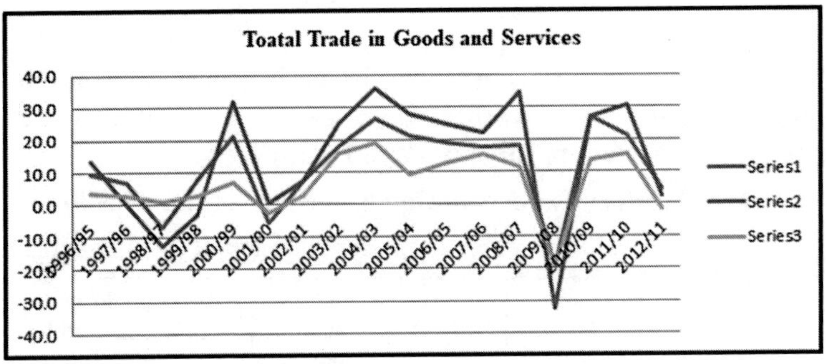

Figure 4.6: Region-wise International Trade in Goods and Services (Exports), 1995-2012

Note: Series 1 - Developing Economies, Series 2 - Transition Economies, Series 3 - Developed Economies

Source: Based on Table 4.2

This shows that in contrast to trade in goods, the trade in services has experienced less diversion in favour of developing and transition economies. However, the comparatively high trend growth rates of 10.9 per cent of developing economies and 13.6 per cent of transition economies as compared to 8.3 per of developed economies during the period of study demonstrates changes in favour of these economies. Therefore, it is evident from the discussion that developed economies still dominate and lead in trade in services in the world market and considered to be a challenge for the developing and transition economies.

4.4 India's Foreign Trade: Goods and Services

Over the period, the external sector of Indian economy has undergone significant transformation. Under the new regime of liberalisation, privatisation and globalisation, the foreign trade of India economy has been playing a strategic role in the process of economic development (Singh, 2000). Further, India's trade relations and participation in international trade with all the regions of the world have increased over the years and this has been largely influenced by the healthy economic environment for international trade in the world. Developing and emerging economies of the world, including India is expected to improve their participation and share in world trade, in view of liberal trade policies being pursued by these countries. In this background, it is important to study the international trade of India. The overview of world trade of India in goods and services has been presented in Table 4.3 and Figure 4.7.

Table 4.3 India's Exports of Goods and Services, 1995-2012

(US $ Millions at current prices and current exchange rate)

Year	Goods	Share in World Exports of Goods	Services	Share in World Exports of Services	Total	Share in World Total Exports
1995	31239 (82.2)	0.6	6775 (17.8)	0.6	38013 (100)	0.6
1996	33737 (82.3)	0.6	7238 (17.7)	0.5	40976	0.6
1997	35702 (79.7)	0.6	9111 (20.3)	0.7	44813	0.6
1998	34076 (74.5)	0.6	11691 (25.5)	0.8	45767	0.7
1999	36877 (71.8)	0.6	14509 (28.2)	1.0	51386	0.7
2000	43247 (72.2)	0.7	16685 (27.8)	1.1	59932	0.8

Year	Goods	Share in World Exports of Goods	Services	Share in World Exports of Services	Total	Share in World Total Exports
2001	44793 (72.1)	0.7	17337 (27.9)	1.1	62130	0.8
2002	51141 (72.4)	0.8	19478 (27.6)	1.2	70619	0.9
2003	60893 (71.8)	0.8	23902 (28.2)	1.3	84795	0.9
2004	77939 (67.1)	0.9	38281 (32.9)	1.7	116220	1.0
2005	102176 (66.0)	1.0	52527 (34.0)	2.0	154703	1.2
2006	123768 (64.0)	1.0	69730 (36.0)	2.4	193498	1.3
2007	153784 (63.9)	1.1	86929 (36.1)	2.5	240713	1.4
2008	198598 (65.0)	1.2	107131 (35.0)	2.7	305729	1.5
2009	168305 (64.5)	1.4	92542 (35.5)	2.6	260847	1.6
2010	231089 (66.4)	1.5	116946 (33.6)	3.0	348035	1.8
2011	307621 (68.9)	1.7	138754 (31.1)	3.2	446375	2.0
2012	297486 (67.1)	1.6	146144 (32.9)	3.3	443629 (100)	2.0
TGR	16.1	–	22.0	–	17.7	–

Note: 1. TGR - Trend Growth Rate. 2. Figures in parenthesis are percentages

Source: UNCTADSTAT, United Nations Conference on Trade and Development Statistics

In India's overall exports, the share of exports of goods was around 82 per cent and that of services about 18 per cent in 1995. During post WTO period, the share of exports of goods has declined to around 67 per cent and that of exports of services has increased to around 33 per cent during 2012. During the period 1995-2012, exports of services has registered 22 per cent trend growth rate, followed by 17.7 per cent in case of overall exports and 16.1 per cent of exports of goods alone. The annual percentage changes in the share of goods exports, share of services exports and India's total exports during the period of study has also been plotted and shown in figure 4.7. It is clear that services exports have witnessed highest annual percentage change during 1995-2012. The position of India's exports of goods, services and total trade with respect to international exports of goods, services and total trade reveals that share of India has increased during period 1995-2012. The share of exports of goods of India in World goods exports was 0.6 per cent in 1995 and it has increased to 1.6 per cent in 2012. The share of exports of services of India in World services exports was 0.6 per cent in 1995 and it has increased around six times to 3.3 per cent in 2012. Similarly, the share of India's share of exports in World exports has increased from 0.6 per cent in 1995 to 2 per cent in 2012.

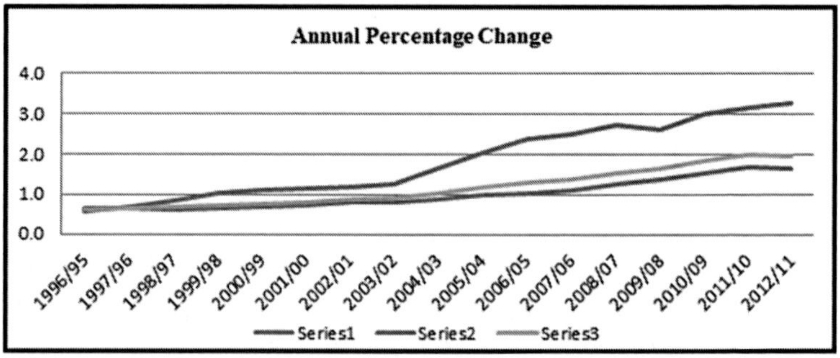

Figure 4.7: India's Exports of Goods, Services and Total Trade, 1995-2012

Note: Series 1 - goods, Series 2 - services, Series 3 - total goods and services

Source: Based on Table 4.3

The analysis and discussion regarding the shares of exports of goods and services in total exports of India clearly shows that exports of services have been emerging future area of exports for India. It can be safely concluded on the basis of four indicators, share of India's services exports in total exports of India, share of services exports of India in world services exports, annual percentage change of services exports of India and comparatively high growth rate of services share in India's export that services exports seems to be the future growth engine of Indian economy.

4.5 Services Trade of India, BRICS and SAARC: Growth and Performance

Since early 1990s the international trade in services has been the fastest growing component of international trade and the composition of services trade has shifted dramatically in favour of high-skill intensive categories of services. Recently, the volume of global trade in services stood at US $ 4645 billion and has been growing at an average annual growth rate of 6 per cent (WTO, 2014). The growing contribution of the services sector in economic growth, employment, and trade has been a key factor in the economic transformation and structural change across the globe. The growing importance and emerging trends in service sectors of developed and developing economies have generated debate regarding the international trade in services and now it is a key issue in world trade agreements and negotiations. India is among the fast growing economies of the world and its services sector has been a major contributor to GDP, economic growth and largest employer after agriculture (Bhattacharya and Mitra 1990). The growth of India's services sector and its increasing share in trade and investment has attracted attention of global players. The literature shows that the growth of services sector has been the result of new economic policies of liberalisation, privatisation and globalisation, and reforms of the 1990s (Jain and Ninan, 2010). During economic reforms period, India witnessed a change in demand pattern from necessary to discretionary consumptions like education, business, personal and health care services. Over the period of time, the developed countries have started outsourcing of services to developing countries like India, BRICS and SAARC, leading to a rise in demand for services from the developing market (Hansda, 2001). Also, the increased public spending in India on certain services like community, social and personal services has led to high growth of services (Ansari, 1995). Further, globalisation facilitates the knowledge generation and spill over, technological progress and availability of high skilled manpower, which has led to growth of professional and commercial services like IT and IT-enabled services (Chanda, 2002). Therefore, in this light, it is important to probe the volume, growth and trends of services exports of India, BRICS and SAARC.

4.5.1 *Services Exports of India, BRICS and SAARC: Volume, Share and Growth*

The overview of exports of goods and services has clearly brought out that the volume, share and growth of exports are crucial and important for the growth of GDP and employment in any economy. In this section of the chapter, an attempt has been made to analyse India's exports of services, exports of services of Brazil, Russia, India, China and South Africa (BRICS) and South Asian Association for Regional Cooperation (SAARC) countries. The information in this regard of BRICS countries and SAARC countries has been shown in Table 4.4 and Table 4.5 respectively.

Table 4.4: BRICS Exports of Services, 1995-2012

(US $ Millions at current prices and current exchange rate)

Year	Brazil	Russia	India	China	South Africa	BRICS
1995	6135 (12.9)	10781 (22.7)	6775 (14.3)	19130 (40.3)	4619 (9.7)	47440 (100)
1996	4655 (9.1)	13550 (26.5)	7238 (14.2)	20601 (40.3)	5069 (9.9)	51113 (100)
1997	5989 (10.1)	14364 (24.2)	9111 (15.3)	24569 (41.3)	5394 (9.1)	59427 (100)
1998	7631 (12.5)	12622 (20.6)	11691 (19.1)	23895 (39.0)	5396 (8.8)	61235 (100)
1999	7189 (11.5)	9250 (14.8)	14509 (23.2)	26248 (42.1)	5210 (8.3)	62406 (100)
2000	9498 (13.3)	9758 (13.7)	16685 (23.4)	30431 (42.6)	5046 (7.1)	71418 (100)
2001	9322 (12.2)	11442 (15.0)	17337 (22.7)	33334 (43.7)	4845 (6.4)	76280 (100)

Year	Brazil	Russia	India	China	South Africa	BRICS
2002	9551 (10.9)	13611 (15.6)	19478 (22.3)	39745 (45.5)	4985 (5.7)	87370 (100)
2003	10447 (9.9)	16229 (15.3)	23903 (22.6)	46760 (44.2)	8440 (8.0)	105779 (100)
2004	12584 (8.6)	20595 (14.1)	38281 (26.2)	64913 (44.4)	9873 (6.8)	146246 (100)
2005	16048 (9.0)	24970 (13.9)	52527 (29.3)	74404 (41.5)	11300 (6.3)	179249 (100)
2006	19462 (8.7)	31102 (13.9)	69730 (31.1)	92006 (41.0)	12214 (5.4)	224514 (100)
2007	23954 (8.4)	39257 (13.7)	86929 (30.4)	122206 (42.7)	13818 (4.8)	286164 (100)
2008	30451 (8.7)	51178 (14.7)	107131 (30.7)	147110 (42.2)	12805 (3.7)	348675 (100)
2009	27728 (9.1)	42411 (13.9)	92542 (30.4)	129476 (42.6)	12020 (4.0)	304177 (100)
2010	31599 (8.5)	45080 (12.2)	116946 (31.6)	162165 (43.9)	14004 (3.8)	369794 (100)
2011	38209 (9.0)	55227 (13.0)	138754 (32.8)	176422 (41.7)	14824 (3.5)	423436 (100)
2012	39864 (8.8)	59104 (13.1)	146144 (32.4)	191430 (42.4)	15148 (3.4)	451690 (100)
TGR	13.7	12.1	22.0	16.4	8.6	16.1

Note: 1. TRG - Trend Growth Rate. 2. Figures in parenthesis are percentages

Source: UNCTADSTAT, United Nations Conference on Trade and Development Statistics

Analysis of exports of services of BRICS countries shows that the share of Brazil declined from 12.9 per cent in 1995 to 8.8 per cent in 2012. The share of Russia and South Africa has also declined from 22.7 per cent and 9.7 per cent in 1995 to 13.1 per cent and 3.4 per cent in 2012 respectively. However, the share of India in exports of services has increased from 14.3 per cent in 1995 to 32.4 per cent in 2012. China managed a constant share of exports of services, over 40 per cent with marginal increase during same period. During the post-liberalisation of trade period BRICS countries has registered 16.1 per cent trend growth of exports of services. The analysis in this regard shows that during the period of study, among the BRICS countries India has registered the highest annual growth rate of 22 per cent in exports of services. It is followed by China (16.4 per cent), Brazil (13.7 per cent), Russia (12.8 per cent) and South Africa (8.6 per cent). It clearly emerged from the above discussed indicators of exports in services of BRICS countries that losses of share in exports of services of Brazil, Russia and South Africa has been largely absorbed by India and marginally by China. Further, it is also evident that though the share of exports of services of BRICS countries shifted in favour of others but all the BRICS countries has registered satisfactory trend rates of growth over the period of study. From this it can be safely concluded that India is emerging as a hub of services exports among BRICS countries.

Analysis of services exports of SAARC countries shows that the share of Bangladesh, Maldives, Nepal, Pakistan and Sri Lanka has declined from 6.3 per cent, 2.1 per cent, 6.1 per cent, 16.8 per cent and 7.4 per cent respectively in 1995 to 1.6 per cent, 1.2 per cent, 0.6 per cent, 4 per cent and 2.3 per cent in 2012 respectively. During the same period the share of services exports of Bhutan in SAARC countries remained constant at 0.1 per cent throughout the study period. However, the share of exports of services of India in SAARC countries increased from 61.2 per cent in 1995 to 88.4 per cent in 2012. Afghanistan on the other hand registered a decline in share of exports of services from 1.8 per cent in 2009 to 1.1 per cent in 2012. The analysis shows that during 1995-2012 services exports of Bangladesh, Maldives, Nepal, Pakistan and Sri Lanka registered decline and services exports of India for the same period managed to grow at a good rate. During the period 1995-2012, the SAARC countries as whole have registered a trend growth rate of 19.4 per cent in services exports. The highest trend growth rate of

22 per cent in the exports of services over the same period was recorded by India. It was followed by Bhutan with 13.3 per cent, Maldives with 13 per cent, Bangladesh with 9.5 per cent, Pakistan with 9.5 per cent, Sri Lanka with 8.7 per cent and the lowest trend growth rate was registered by Nepal with 0.8 per cent. It is pertinent to mention that Nepal was the only country in SAARC who suffered huge loss of share in exports of services; it slipped from 6.1 per cent in 1995 to 0.6 per cent in 2012, this may be due the insecurity and political uncertainty during the same period. Pakistan's exports of services among the SAARC remained at second position after India during the period of study. Afghanistan registered a trend growth rate of 16.6 per cent during the period 2009-12. Further, it is also evident that though the share of exports of services of SAARC countries shifted in favour of others but, all the SAARC countries has registered positive trend rates of growth over the period of study. Again from the analysis and discussion it can be concluded that India is emerging as a hub of services exports among SAARC countries as well.

India's exports of services among the BRICS and SAARC countries during post-WTO period suggest that it has emerged as an important origin and hub of service producing country. Therefore, it is suggested that India must invest in the service sector to build world class infrastructure and facilities to attract the service demand from every corner of the world. For the purpose, right and comprehensive policy measures and political will should be in place to cope up with revolution of services of the developed countries.

Table 4.5: SAARC Exports of Services, 1995-2012

(US $ Millions at current prices and current exchange rate)

Year	Afghanistan	Bangladesh	Bhutan	India	Maldives	Nepal	Pakistan	Sri Lanka	SAARC
1995	–	698 (6.3)	15 (0.1)	6775 (61.2)	233 (2.1)	679 (6.1)	1857 (16.8)	819 (7.4)	11077 (100)
1996	–	605 (5.2)	10 (0.1)	7238 (62.0)	289 (2.5)	757 (6.5)	2016 (17.3)	765 (6.5)	11682 (100)
1997	–	687 (5.1)	16 (0.1)	9111 (67.5)	312 (2.3)	866 (6.4)	1625 (12.0)	875 (6.5)	13493 (100)

Year	Afghanistan	Bangladesh	Bhutan	India	Maldives	Nepal	Pakistan	Sri Lanka	SAARC
1998	–	724 (4.6)	15 (0.1)	11691 (74.7)	331 (2.1)	565 (3.6)	1404 (9.0)	917 (5.9)	15647 (100)
1999	–	778 (4.2)	18 (0.1)	14509 (77.8)	343 (1.8)	655 (3.5)	1373 (7.4)	964 (5.2)	18640 (100)
2000	–	815 (3.9)	20 (0.1)	16685 (80.6)	348 (1.7)	506 (2.4)	1380 (6.7)	939 (4.5)	20694 (100)
2001	–	752 (3.5)	24 (0.1)	17337 (79.9)	354 (1.6)	413 (1.9)	1459 (6.7)	1355 (6.2)	21695 (100)
2002	–	849 (3.4)	23 (0.1)	19478 (78.6)	363 (1.5)	305 (1.2)	2429 (9.8)	1268 (5.1)	24766 (100)
2003	–	1012 (3.4)	20 (0.1)	23903 (79.2)	432 (1.4)	372 (1.2)	2968 (9.8)	1411 (4.7)	30199 (100)
2004	–	1083 (2.4)	28 (0.1)	38281 (85.6)	508 (1.1)	461 (1.0)	2749 (6.1)	1527 (3.4)	44717 (100)
2005	–	1249 (2.1)	42 (0.1)	52527 (87.8)	323 (0.5)	380 (0.6)	3678 (6.1)	1540 (2.6)	59847 (100)
2006	–	1334 (1.7)	52 (0.1)	69730 (90.2)	552 (0.7)	386 (0.5)	3506 (4.5)	1625 (2.1)	77291 (100)
2007	–	1617 (1.7)	60 (0.1)	86929 (91.1)	649 (0.7)	511 (0.5)	3767 (3.9)	1775 (1.9)	95415 (100)
2008	–	1996 (1.7)	55 (0.1)	107131 (91.6)	721 (0.6)	724 (0.6)	4263 (3.6)	2002 (1.7)	116998 (100)
2009	1894 (1.8)	1975 (1.9)	56 (0.1)	92542 (88.5)	1543 (1.5)	705 (0.7)	3967 (3.8)	1892 (1.8)	104575 (100)
2010	3140 (2.3)	2412 (1.8)	69 (0.1)	116946 (87.2)	1810 (1.3)	672 (0.5)	6588 (4.9)	2474 (1.8)	134110 (100)
2011	3476 (2.2)	2423 (1.6)	82 (0.1)	138754 (89.1)	2005 (1.3)	863 (0.6)	5035 (3.2)	3084 (2.0)	155721 (100)
2012	3056 (1.8)	2642 (1.6)	102	146144 (88.4)	2016 (1.2)	925 (0.6)	6600 (4.0)	3800 (2.3)	165284 (100)
TGR	16.6	9.5	13.3	22.0	13.0	0.8	9.5	8.7	19.4

Note: 1. TGR - Trend Growth Rate. 2. Figures in parenthesis are percentages

Source: UNCTADSTAT, United Nations Conference on Trade and Development Statistics

4.6 Services Exports of India, SAARC, BRICS and World: Composition

Composition of Indian exports has registered a number of structural changes over the period. There has been a decline in the share of agriculture and allied products and a substantial increase in the share of manufactured products and services. Further, the increasing service exports since 1991 has also witnessed changes in composition of service exports of India. Services exports of India comprised of travel and tourism, IT and software, financial and business, educational, health and many other commercial services. Therefore, it is important to investigate the composition of India's, BRICS's and SAARC's services exports. For the purpose, the study period has been divided into two sub-periods according to classification of services category by UNCTAD, during first period 1995-99, the services has been classified into three categories as travel, transport, other commercial services and total services. The services during second period 2000-12 has been classified into eleven different categories like communications, telecommunication, construction, insurance, financial services, computer and information services, computer services, royalties and license fees, other business services, personal, cultural and recreational services, audiovisual and related services, and government services.

4.6.1 *Composition During 1995-1999*

The relevant information of the composition of services exports of world, India, BRICS and SAARC countries during 1995-99 has been presented in Table 4.6.

Table 4.6: Category-wise Services Exports of World, SAARC, BRICS and India, 1995-1999

(US $ Millions at current prices and current exchange rate)

Year	Total Services	Transport Services	Travel Services	Other Services
WORLD				
1995	1222220 (100)	310120 (25.4)	397870 (32.6)	506640 (41.5)
1996	1317310 (100)	315950 (24.0)	433450 (32.9)	563610 (42.8)
1997	1372610 (100)	326110 (23.8)	437700 (31.9)	605680 (44.1)

Year	Total Services	Transport Services	Travel Services	Other Services
1998	1389980 (100)	317590 (22.8)	441780 (31.8)	627010 (45.1)
1999	1435550 (100)	324700 (22.6)	459390 (32.0)	651200 (45.4)
SAARC				
1995	11080 (100)	3200 (28.9)	3330 (30.1)	4550 (41.1)
1996	11680 (100)	3280 (28.1)	3560 (30.5)	4830 (41.4)
1997	13490 (100)	3330 (24.7)	3700 (27.4)	6470 (48.0)
1998	15650 (100)	3070 (19.6)	3810 (24.3)	8770 (56.0)
1999	18640 (100)	3170 (17.0)	3900 (20.9)	11570 (62.1)
BRICS				
1995	47440 (100)	12693 (26.8)	18722 (39.5)	16025 (33.8)
1996	51113 (100)	11121 (21.8)	23466 (45.9)	16526 (32.3)
1997	59427 (100)	11041 (18.6)	25956 (43.7)	22432 (37.7)
1998	61235 (100)	10199 (16.7)	26230 (42.8)	24807 (40.5)
1999	62406 (100)	9496 (15.2)	25257 (40.5)	27654 (44.3)
India				
1995	6775 (100)	1890 (27.9)	2582 (38.1)	2303 (34.0)
1996	7238 (100)	1989 (27.5)	2831 (39.1)	2418 (33.4)
1997	9111 (100)	1942 (21.3)	2890 (31.7)	4279 (47.0)
1998	11691 (100)	1773 (15.2)	2949 (25.2)	6970 (59.6)

Year	Total Services	Transport Services	Travel Services	Other Services
1999	14509 (100)	1844 (12.7)	3010 (20.7)	9656 (66.6)

Note: Figures in parenthesis are percentages

Source: UNCTADSTAT, United Nations Conference on Trade and Development Statistics

The analysis of total services exports of the world shows that in 1995 about 25 per cent were exports of transport services, about 33 were travel services and about 42 per cent other commercial services. The respective shares of transport services, travel services and other commercial services during 1995-99 almost remained the same and experienced little change in favour of other services exports. However, the category-wise services exports of SAARC countries have witnessed sharp changes during 1995-99 in favour of other services. The respective shares of exports of transport and travel services have declined from about 29 per cent and about 30 per cent in 1995 to around 17 per cent and about 21 per cent in 1999. In the case of BRICS countries, the share of transport services exports has declined from about 27 per cent in 1995 to around 15 per cent in 1999. But the exports of travel services have remained same around 40 per cent of the services exports during 1995-99. The decline of exports of transport services has been captured by other services exports as they have shot up to around 44 per cent in 1999 from about 34 per cent in 1995. Exports of travel and transport services of India experienced a steep decline during 1995-99 and exports of other services has been doubled during the same period. The data shows that exports of transport and travel services of India decreased from about 28 per cent and around 38 per cent in 1995 to about 13 per cent and 21 per cent in 1999 respectively. However, the exports of other services has increased from about 34 per cent in 1995 to around 67 per cent in 1999 in total exports of services of India.

Above analysis of exports of different categories of services of India, SAARC, BRICS and world clearly depicts that the shares of travel and transport services have declined and that of exports of other services experienced a rise during immediate post-WTO period 1995-99. It also evidently emerged that this shift has been the result of liberalisation of trade especially trade in services and introduction of modern services and commercialisation of services across the countries.

4.6.2 *Composition During 2000-2012*

The information and data of exports of services like communications, telecommunication, construction, insurance, financial services, computer and information services, computer services, royalties and license fees, other business services, personal, cultural and recreational services, audiovisual and related services, and government services of world, SAARC, BRICS and India during second period 2000-12 has been presented in Table 4.7, Table 4.8, Table 4.9 and Table 4.10 and depicted in Figure 4.8, Figure 4.9, Figure 4.10 and Figure 4.11 respectively.

The analysis of total world exports of services during period 2000-12 has registered 10.7 per cent annual trend growth rate. The share of exports of travel services in world services exports was highest at 31.3 per cent followed by exports of transport services (22.8 per cent), other business services (21.4 per cent), financial services (6.4 per cent) and royalties and license fees (6 per cent) in world exports of services in 2000. The combined share of communication services, construction services, insurance services, computer and information, personal, cultural and recreational services, and government services was around about 12 per cent of the world exports of services in 2000. The analysis of exports of different services during the period 2000-12 reveals that the share of these services exports remained almost same in the total world services exports. To evaluate the growth of different categories of services exports, the 10.7 per cent growth rate of total world services exports during the period 2000-12, has been considered as a benchmark growth rate for different

Table 4.7: Category-wise Services Exports of World, 2000-2012

(US $ Millions at current prices and current exchange rate)

Service Code → ↓ Year	TS	01	02	07	06	16	13	10	14	15	18	21
2000	1521980 (100)	346370 (22.8)	476820 (31.3)	34300 (2.3)	30200 (2.0)	27710 (1.8)	97580 (6.4)	45650 (3.0)	91930 (6.0)	325890 (21.4)	14650 (1.0)	30660 (2.0)
2001	1525110 (100)	339180 (22.2)	467300 (30.6)	36350 (2.4)	31620 (2.1)	29840 (2.0)	93520 (6.1)	53150 (3.5)	90470 (5.9)	338180 (22.2)	12920 (0.8)	32380 (2.1)
2002	1634070 (100)	354710 (21.7)	487180 (29.8)	37420 (2.3)	35300 (2.2)	44380 (2.7)	99910 (6.1)	59080 (3.6)	98610 (6.0)	364680 (22.3)	15980 (1.0)	36490 (2.2)
2003	1896590 (100)	400810 (21.1)	544630 (28.7)	45030 (2.4)	39610 (2.1)	54250 (2.9)	120200 (6.3)	74970 (4.0)	115780 (6.1)	437450 (23.1)	18350 (1.0)	45220 (2.4)
2004	2302350 (100)	502010 (21.8)	649990 (28.2)	53820 (2.3)	46380 (2.0)	56550 (2.5)	153400 (6.7)	93410 (4.1)	141490 (6.1)	528340 (22.9)	22840 (1.0)	51930 (2.3)
2005	2573220 (100)	569280 (22.1)	703010 (27.3)	59400 (2.3)	56050 (2.2)	49400 (1.9)	180550 (7.0)	103820 (4.0)	159690 (6.2)	609370 (23.7)	23280 (0.9)	57040 (2.2)
2006	2908700 (100)	635740 (21.9)	761490 (26.2)	71310 (2.5)	68970 (2.4)	62200 (2.1)	225270 (7.7)	125510 (4.3)	173790 (6.0)	695190 (23.9)	23750 (0.8)	63280 (2.2)

Service Code → ↓ Year	TS	01	02	07	06	16	13	10	14	15	18	21
2007	3490240 (100)	766130 (22.0)	875960 (25.1)	83010 (2.4)	86540 (2.5)	76730 (2.2)	297280 (8.5)	156120 (4.5)	204090 (5.8)	844390 (24.2)	26780 (0.8)	688890 (2.0)
2008	3916200 (100)	890670 (22.7)	963200 (24.6)	97700 (2.5)	112150 (2.9)	83490 (2.1)	298620 (7.6)	195190 (5.0)	228740 (5.8)	944850 (24.1)	29300 (0.7)	69140 (1.8)
2009	3555580 (100)	692820 (19.5)	876570 (24.7)	93450 (2.6)	109320 (3.1)	96100 (2.7)	262930 (7.4)	189950 (5.3)	236260 (6.6)	899550 (25.3)	27800 (0.8)	66890 (1.9)
2010	3896060 (100)	807470 (20.7)	951500 (24.4)	97160 (2.5)	99410 (2.6)	96720 (2.5)	282110 (7.2)	213810 (5.5)	255470 (6.6)	983670 (25.2)	33010 (0.8)	68580 (1.8)
2011	4372890 (100)	880140 (20.1)	1064510 (24.3)	106340 (2.4)	106580 (2.4)	105300 (2.4)	316870 (7.2)	249530 (5.7)	290270 (6.6)	1128780 (25.8)	38620 (0.9)	77480 (1.8)
2012	4473810 (100)	888450 (19.9)	1104230 (24.7)	111160 (2.5)	107010 (2.4)	104160 (2.3)	308470 (6.9)	261370 (5.8)	293470 (6.6)	1172740 (26.2)	39470 (0.9)	76810 (1.7)
TGR	10.7	9.7	8.2	11.6	13.5	11.8	12.4	16.6	11.6	12.4	9.3	8.2

Note: 1. TGR - Trend Growth Rate, 2. Figures in parenthesis are percentages, 3. TS - Total Service, 01 - Transport, 02 - Travel, 07 - Communication, 06 - Construction, 16 - Insurance, 13 - Financial services, 10 - Computer and Information, 14 - Royalties and License Fees, 15 - Other Business services, 18 - Personal, Cultural and Recreational services, 21 - Government services

Source: UNCTADSTAT, United Nations Conference on Trade and Development Statistics, 2014

services during the same period. During the period 2000-12, the non-traditional and newly emerged services exports like IT, communication, construction, insurance, financial services, computer and information, royalties and license fees, and other business services have registered comparatively higher growth rates. But on the other hand traditional services exports like transport, travel, personal, cultural and recreational services, and government services grew at a rate below the benchmark growth rate during the same period.

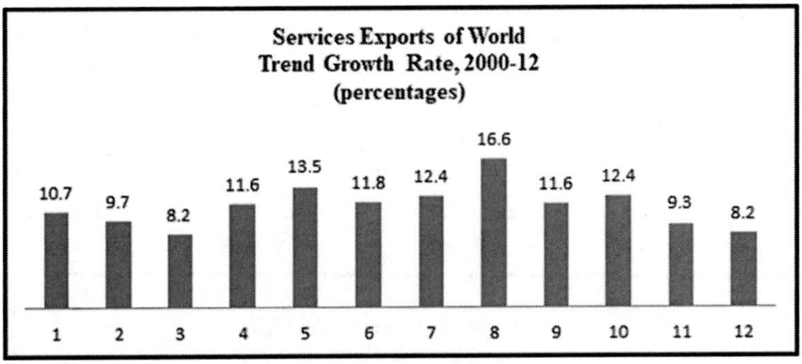

Figure 4.8: Growth of Services Exports of World, 2000-2012

Note: 1 - Total services (TS), 2 - Transport (01), 3 - Travel (02), 4 - Communication (07), 5 - Construction (06), 6 - Insurance (16), 7 - Financial services (13), 8 - Computer and Information (10), 9 - Royalties and License Fees (14), 10 - Other Business services (15), 11 - Personal, Cultural and Recreational services (18), 12 - Government services (21)

Source: Based on Table 4.7

The analysis shows that the annual growth rate of total services exports of SAARC countries has been 21.3 per cent during 2000-2012. In SAARC countries, the highest share of 25.5 per cent in services exports in the year 2000 was of other business services, followed by travel services (20.9 per cent), computer and information services (19.8 per cent), transport services (16.4 per cent), and government services (6.8 per cent). The combined share of communication services, construction services, insurance services, financial services and personal, cultural and recreational services is around 10 per cent of the total services exports of SAARC countries. During the period 2000-12, the shares of other business services and computer and information services in total services exports of SAARC countries have swelled from 25.6 per cent and 19.8 per cent in 2000 to 30.7 per cent and 29.1 per cent in 2012 respectively. Transport and travel services on the other hand have witnessed a decline in their share in total services exports of SAARC countries from 16.4 per cent and 20.9 per cent in 2000 to 12.9 per cent and 13.2 per cent in 2012. The shares of the remaining services remained almost the same during the period 2000-12. Again, the 21.3 per cent trend growth rate of the total services exports is considered as the benchmark for the evaluation of growth of various services exports of SAARC countries during 2000-12. Similarly as in case of services exports of the world, the non-traditional and modern services

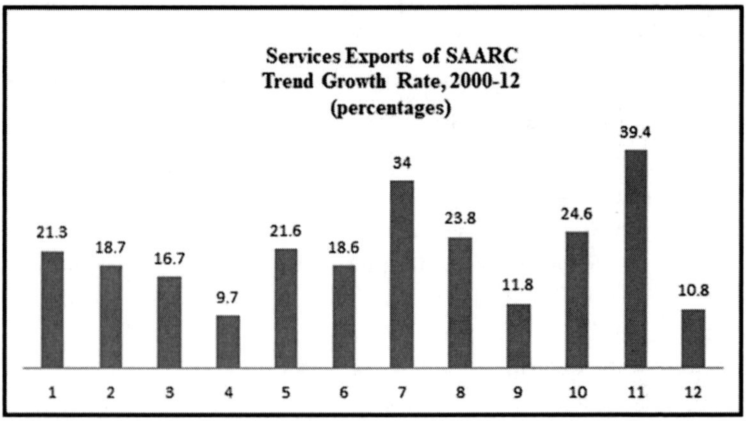

Figure 4.9: Growth of Services Exports of SAARC, 2000-2012

Note: 1 - Total Services (TS), 2 - Transport (01), 3 - Travel (02), 4 - Communication (07), 5 - Construction (06), 6 - Insurance (16), 7 - Financial services (13), 8 - Computer and Information (10), 9 - Royalties and License Fees (14), 10 - Other Business services (15), 11 - Personal, Cultural and Recreational services (18), 12 - Government services (21)

Source: Based on Table 4.8

Table 4.8: Category-wise Services Exports of SAARC, 2000-2012

(US $ Millions at current prices and current exchange rate)

Service Code → ↓ Year	TS	01	02	07	06	16	13	10	14	15	18	21
2000	20690 (100)	3400 (16.4)	4320 (20.9)	870 (4.2)	530 (2.6)	310 (1.5)	330 (1.6)	4090 (19.8)	–	5290 (25.6)	20 (0.1)	1400 (6.8)
2001	21700 (100)	3400 (15.7)	4020 (18.5)	1360 (6.3)	110 (0.5)	730 (3.4)	360 (1.7)	6040 (27.8)	–	4240 (19.5)	20 (0.1)	1340 (6.2)
2002	24770 (100)	3950 (15.9)	4080 (16.5)	1230 (5.0)	280 (1.1)	400 (1.6)	650 (2.6)	6660 (26.9)	–	5470 (22.1)	30 (0.1)	1970 (8.0)
2003	30200 (100)	4580 (15.2)	5710 (18.9)	1300 (4.3)	340 (1.1)	480 (1.6)	440 (1.5)	8670 (28.7)	–	6110 (20.2)	40 (0.1)	2470 (8.2)
2004	44720 (100)	6100 (13.6)	7660 (17.1)	1460 (3.3)	590 (1.3)	920 (2.1)	430 (1.0)	12260 (27.4)	–	12990 (29.0)	50 (0.1)	2170 (4.9)
2005	59850 (100)	7710 (12.9)	8630 (14.4)	1960 (3.3)	430 (0.7)	1060 (1.8)	1240 (2.1)	16250 (27.2)	–	19310 (32.3)	120 (0.2)	2870 (4.8)
2006	77290 (100)	9620 (12.4)	10070 (13.0)	2510 (3.2)	720 (0.9)	1200 (1.6)	2480 (3.2)	21580 (27.9)	150 (0.2)	26200 (33.9)	310 (0.4)	2430 (3.1)

Service Code → ↓ Year	TS	01	02	07	06	16	13	10	14	15	18	21
2007	95410 (100)	11140 (11.7)	12330 (12.9)	2670 (2.8)	900 (0.9)	1610 (1.7)	3510 (3.7)	27800 (29.1)	230 (0.2)	31710 (33.2)	510 (0.5)	3000 (3.1)
2008	117000 (100)	14020 (12.0)	13630 (11.6)	2810 (2.4)	960 (0.8)	1720 (1.5)	4420 (3.8)	36330 (31.1)	230 (0.2)	38710 (33.1)	720 (0.6)	3470 (3.0)
2009	104570 (100)	13350 (12.8)	13790 (13.2)	2670 (2.6)	1580 (1.5)	1650 (1.6)	4080 (3.9)	32810 (31.4)	230 (0.2)	29060 (27.8)	460 (0.4)	3040 (2.9)
2010	134110 (100)	16330 (12.2)	17600 (13.1)	2470 (1.8)	1660 (1.2)	1920 (1.4)	6480 (4.8)	39530 (29.5)	170 (0.1)	36960 (27.6)	360 (0.3)	5540 (4.1)
2011	155720 (100)	21410 (13.7)	21350 (13.7)	2690 (1.7)	2100 (1.3)	2830 (1.8)	6690 (4.3)	46170 (29.6)	360 (0.2)	41850 (26.9)	360 (0.2)	3480 (2.2)
2012	165280 (100)	21370 (12.9)	21790 (13.2)	2710 (1.6)	1820 (1.1)	2540 (1.5)	5640 (3.4)	48130 (29.1)	350 (0.2)	50800 (30.7)	780 (0.5)	5460 (3.3)
TGR	21.3	18.7	16.7	9.7	21.6	18.6	34.0	23.8	11.8	24.6	39.4	10.8

Note: 1. TGR - Trend Growth Rate, 2. Figures in parenthesis are percentages, 3. TS - Total Service, 01 - Transport, 02 - Travel, 07 - Communication, 06 - Construction, 16 - Insurance, 13 - Financial services, 10 - Computer and Information, 14- Royalties and License Fees, 15 - Other Business services, 18 - Personal, Cultural and Recreational services, 21 - Government services

Source: UNCTADSTAT, United Nations Conference on Trade and Development Statistics, 2014

like construction services, financial services, computer and information services and other business services have reported comparatively higher growth rates. However, the personal, cultural and recreational service was the only traditional service category that registered the highest growth rate of 39.4 per cent during the period 2000-12. The remaining services such as transport services, travel services, insurance services, royalties and license fee services, and government services grew at a rate below the benchmark growth rate during the same period.

The analysis shows that the trend growth rate of the total services exports of the BRICS countries was 18.4 per cent during the period 2000-12. In the year 2000, travel services exports has reported the highest share of 38.7 per cent, followed by other business services (20.2 per cent), transport services (16.5 per cent) share and computer and information services (6.3 per cent) share in total services exports of BRICS countries. The combined share of communication services, construction services, insurance services, financial services, royalties and license fee services, personal, cultural and recreational services and government services was around 12 per cent in the same year. Other business services and computer and information services

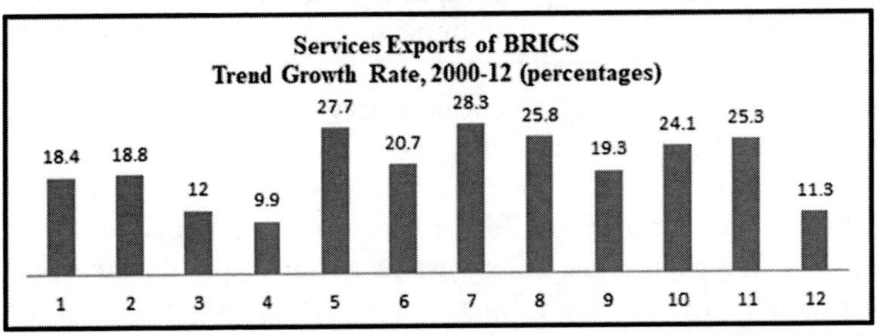

Figure 4.10: Growth of Services Exports of BRICS, 2000-2012

Note: 1 - Total services (TS), 2 - Transport (01), 3 - Travel (02), 4 - Communication (07), 5 - Construction (06), 6 - Insurance (16), 7 - Financial services (13), 8 - Computer and Information (10), 9 - Royalties and License Fees (14), 10 - Other Business services (15), 11 - Personal, Cultural and Recreational services (18), 12 - Government services (21)

Source: Based on Table 4.9

registered the highest increase in their share in total services exports of BRICS countries from 20.2 per cent and 6.3 per cent in 2000 to 34.1 per cent and 14.3 per cent in 2012. The share of remaining services remained almost the same during the period 2000-12. As in the cases of world and SAARC countries exports of services, the 18.4 per cent trend growth rate of total services of the BRICS countries during the period 2000-12 is considered as yardstick for evaluating the growth of various services. Under this criterion, the transport services, construction services, insurance services, financial services, computer and information services, royalties and license fee services and personal, cultural and recreational services registered a higher trend growth rate than the benchmark trend growth rate. On the other hand, the travel services, communication services and government services grew at a lower trend growth rate than the benchmark trend growth rate during the period 2000-12.

The analysis of the total services exports of India shows that the annual growth rate of total services exports was 22.7 per cent during the post WTO and GATS period 2000-12. In the year 2000 computer and information services had the highest share of 24.3 per cent followed by travel services (20.7 per cent), and transport services (11.9 per cent) in the services exports of India. The combined share of communication services, construction services, insurance services, financial services, royalties and license fee services, other business services, personal, cultural and recreational services and government services was almost about 14 per cent. The analysis reveals that during the period 2000-12 the shares of different services remained almost the same in the total services exports of India. Applying the same formula for India, the 22.7 per cent annual growth rate of total services exports as the standard growth rate for all services for the period 2000-12, analysis reveals that the annual growth rate of computer and information services and personal, cultural and recreational services have registered annual growth rates higher than the benchmark growth rate during the period 2000-12. Transport services and insurance services registered almost the same growth rate as that of the benchmark growth rate. However, the travel services, communication services,

Table 4.9: Category-wise Services Exports of BRICS, 2000-2012

(US $ Millions at current prices and current exchange rate)

Service Code → ↓ Year	TS	01	02	07	06	16	13	10	14	15	18	21
2000	71418 (100)	11797 (16.5)	27607 (38.7)	2422 (3.4)	1502 (2.1)	1163 (1.6)	830 (1.2)	4497 (6.3)	428 (0.6)	14443 (20.2)	74 (0.1)	2380 (3.3)
2001	76280 (100)	13924 (18.3)	28862 (37.8)	2146 (2.8)	1666 (2.2)	814 (1.1)	1090 (1.4)	6609 (8.7)	340 (0.4)	14893 (19.5)	208 (0.3)	2721 (3.6)
2002	87370 (100)	16238 (18.6)	32575 (37.3)	2040 (2.3)	2202 (2.5)	911 (1.0)	1407 (1.6)	7438 (8.5)	419 (0.5)	17180 (19.7)	189 (0.2)	3376 (3.9)
2003	105778 (100)	20130 (19.0)	34562 (32.7)	2635 (2.5)	2647 (2.5)	1096 (1.0)	1353 (1.3)	9934 (9.4)	440 (0.4)	25342 (24.0)	272 (0.3)	4025 (3.8)
2004	146246 (100)	28117 (19.2)	47174 (32.3)	2548 (1.7)	3591 (2.5)	1676 (1.1)	1554 (1.1)	14168 (9.7)	667 (0.5)	44304 (30.3)	386 (0.3)	3881 (2.7)
2005	179249 (100)	34966 (19.5)	54036 (30.1)	3141 (1.8)	5191 (2.9)	2071 (1.2)	2719 (1.5)	18538 (10.3)	770 (0.4)	54711 (30.5)	602 (0.3)	5046 (2.8)
2006	224514 (100)	43585 (19.4)	62647 (27.9)	4187 (1.9)	6485 (2.9)	2521 (1.1)	4535 (2.0)	25177 (11.2)	761 (0.3)	70845 (31.6)	859 (0.4)	5065 (2.3)
2007	286164 (100)	58111 (20.3)	71142 (24.9)	5303 (1.9)	9651 (3.4)	3546 (1.2)	6749 (2.4)	33302 (11.6)	1274 (0.4)	92983 (32.5)	1279 (0.4)	5509 (1.9)

Service Code → ↓ Year	TS	01	02	07	06	16	13	10	14	15	18	21
2008	348675 (100)	71975 (20.6)	78258 (22.4)	6217 (1.8)	15914 (4.6)	4667 (1.3)	7969 (2.3)	44156 (12.7)	1691 (0.5)	112435 (32.2)	1699 (0.5)	6780 (1.9)
2009	304177 (100)	52254 (17.2)	73106 (24.0)	5060 (1.7)	14456 (4.8)	4087 (1.3)	7290 (2.4)	40589 (13.3)	1484 (0.5)	99340 (32.7)	1030 (0.3)	6277 (2.1)
2010	369794 (100)	68783 (18.6)	83921 (22.7)	4775 (1.3)	18600 (5.0)	4626 (1.3)	11118 (3.0)	50111 (13.6)	1799 (0.5)	116053 (31.4)	1060 (0.3)	8924 (2.4)
2011	423436 (100)	78031 (18.4)	93570 (22.1)	5387 (1.3)	20054 (4.7)	6760 (1.6)	11764 (2.8)	59964 (14.2)	2259 (0.5)	133937 (31.6)	1081 (0.3)	7098 (1.7)
2012	451690 (100)	82564 (18.3)	95400 (21.1)	5556 (1.2)	17982 (4.0)	6854 (1.5)	11913 (2.6)	64611 (14.3)	2607 (0.6)	154211 (34.1)	1551 (0.3)	9504 (2.1)
TGR	18.4	18.8	12.0	9.9	27.7	20.7	28.3	25.8	19.3	24.1	25.3	11.3

Note: 1. TRG - Trend Growth Rate, 2. Figures in parenthesis are percentages, 3. TS - Total Service, 01 - Transport, 02 - Travel, 07 - Communication, 06 - Construction, 16 - Insurance, 13 - Financial services, 10 - Computer and Information, 14 - Royalties and License Fees, 15 - Other Business services, 18 - Personal, Cultural and Recreational services, 21 - Government services

Source: UNCTADSTAT, United Nations Conference on Trade and Development Statistics, 2014

construction services, royalties and license fee services, other business services and government services registered a lower growth rate then the benchmark growth rate over the same period.

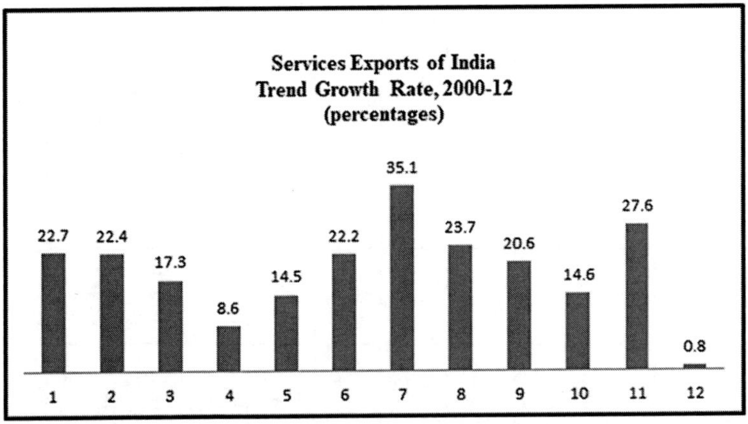

Figure 4.11: Growth of Services Exports of India, 2000-2012

Note: 1 - Total services (TS), 2 - Transport (01), 3 - Travel (02), 4 - Communication (07), 5 - Construction (06), 6 - Insurance (16), 7 - Financial services (13), 8 - Computer and Information (10), 9 - Royalties and License Fees (14), 10 - Other Business services (15), 11 - Personal, Cultural and Recreational services (18), 12 - Government services (21)

Source: Based on Table 4.10

Above analysis of exports of different categories of services of world clearly depicts that the non-traditional and newly emerged services exports like IT, communication, construction, insurance, financial services, computer and information, royalties and license fees, and other business services have emerged stronger and have registered comparatively higher growth rates during post WTO period 2000-12. Similarly in case of SAARC countries, the non-traditional and modern services like construction services, financial services, computer and information services and other business services have reported comparatively higher growth rates. However, the personal, cultural and recreational service was the only traditional service category that remained important during the same period. The

Table 4.10: Category-wise Services Exports of India, 2000-2012

(US $ Millions at current prices and current exchange rate)

Service Code → ↓ Year	TS	01	02	07	06	16	13	10	14	15	18	21
2000	16685 (100)	1979 (11.9)	3460 (20.7)	599 (3.6)	502 (3.0)	257 (1.5)	276 (1.7)	4048 (24.3)	83 (0.5)	–	–	654 (3.9)
2001	17337 (100)	2050 (11.8)	3198 (18.4)	1104 (6.4)	65 (0.4)	282 (1.6)	306 (1.8)	5947 (34.3)	37 (0.2)	–	–	538 (3.1)
2002	19478 (100)	2473 (12.7)	3102 (15.9)	779 (4.0)	231 (1.2)	332 (1.7)	598 (3.1)	6582 (33.8)	20 (0.1)	–	–	353 (1.8)
2003	23902 (100)	3022 (12.6)	4463 (18.7)	969 (4.1)	276 (1.2)	408 (1.7)	367 (1.5)	8562 (35.8)	24 (0.1)	–	–	269 (1.1)
2004	38281 (100)	4373 (11.4)	6170 (16.1)	1094 (2.9)	516 (1.3)	842 (2.2)	341 (0.9)	12133 (31.7)	53 (0.1)	12364 (32.3)	46 (0.1)	350 (0.9)
2005	52527 (100)	5754 (11.0)	7493 (14.3)	1566 (3.0)	346 (0.7)	941 (1.8)	1143 (2.2)	16079 (30.6)	206 (0.4)	18560 (35.3)	111 (0.2)	328 (0.6)
2006	69730 (100)	7561 (10.8)	8634 (12.4)	2181 (3.1)	619 (0.9)	1113 (1.6)	2357 (3.4)	21362 (30.6)	61 (0.1)	25262 (36.2)	306 (0.4)	274 (0.4)

Service Code → ↓ Year	TS	01	02	07	06	16	13	10	14	15	18	21
2007	86929 (100)	9037 (10.4)	10730 (12.3)	2347 (2.7)	753 (0.9)	1506 (1.7)	3379 (3.9)	27476 (31.6)	163 (0.2)	30712 (35.3)	509 (0.6)	317 (0.4)
2008	107131 (100)	11565 (10.8)	11832 (11.0)	2478 (2.3)	841 (0.8)	1561 (1.5)	4291 (4.0)	35868 (33.5)	148 (0.1)	37454 (35.0)	707 (0.7)	386 (0.4)
2009	92542 (100)	10979 (11.9)	11136 (12.0)	1953 (2.1)	809 (0.9)	1515 (1.6)	3617 (3.9)	32332 (34.9)	192 (0.2)	27332 (29.5)	432 (0.5)	405 (0.4)
2010	116946 (100)	13241 (11.3)	14490 (12.4)	1547 (1.3)	526 (0.4)	1781 (1.5)	5834 (5.0)	38996 (33.3)	127 (0.1)	34514 (29.5)	327 (0.3)	485 (0.4)
2011	138754 (100)	17680 (12.7)	17708 (12.8)	1660 (1.2)	838 (0.6)	2584 (1.9)	6249 (4.5)	45474 (32.8)	303 (0.2)	38902 (28.0)	345 (0.2)	593 (0.4)
2012	146144 (100)	17482 (12.0)	17972 (12.3)	1647 (1.1)	922 (0.6)	2258 (1.5)	5135 (3.5)	47178 (32.3)	321 (0.2)	48060 (32.9)	767 (0.5)	495 (0.3)
TGR	22.7	22.4	17.3	8.6	14.5	22.2	35.1	23.7	20.6	14.6	27.6	0.8

Note: 1. TRG - Trend Growth Rate, 2. Figures in parenthesis are percentages, 3. TS - Total Service, 01 - Transport, 02 - Travel, 07 - Communication, 06 - Construction, 16 - Insurance, 13 - Financial services, 10 - Computer and Information, 14 - Royalties and License Fees, 15 - Other Business services, 18 - Personal, Cultural and Recreational services, 21 - Government services

Source: UNCTADSTAT, United Nations Conference on Trade and Development Statistics, 2014

BRICS countries services exports during 2000-12 reveals that the transport services, construction services, insurance services, financial services, computer and information services, royalties and license fee services and personal, cultural and recreational services have emerged as leading services. India's services exports analysis suggests that the computer and information services and personal, cultural and recreational services have major contributors of total services exports during 2000-12. Also, the transport services and insurance services remained significant over the same period. The experiences of exports of services of India, SAARC, BRICS and world during new millennium clearly shows that the shares and growth of traditional services in respective total services exports has dwindled and the shares and growth of non-traditional and newly emerged services has increased. It also evidently emerged from the services exports of India, SAARC, BRICS and world that this shift has been the result of liberalisation of trade especially trade in services and the introduction of modern services and commercialisation of services across the countries.

4.7 Exports of India: Direction

The level of foreign trade is not determined according to comparative advantages, specialisations and composition alone but also by its direction. During pre-independence and immediately after independence period India's direction of foreign trade was mainly towards UK and other European countries. Over the period of time the direction of India's imports as well as exports has drastically changed. India presently has diversified the direction of exports, now USA, Japan, UK and many countries and regions across the globe buy a large volume of goods and services from India. Therefore, it is important to study the direction of exports of India to look at its trading partners. The information of direction of India's exports has been shown in Table 4.11 and Figure 4.12.

The analysis shows that the exports of India to OECD, OPEC, Eastern Europe, developing countries and other unspecified countries have grown at an annual growth rate of 15.8 per cent for the period 1994-95 to 2011-12. The exports to OECD countries and Eastern European countries registered a decline in share from 58.7 per cent and 4.0 per cent in 1994-95 to 33.8 per cent and 1.1 per cent in 2012 respectively. On the other hand, India's exports to OPEC and developing countries registered an increase in the share from 9.2 per cent and 26.5 per cent in 1994-95 to 19.0 per cent and 40.8 per cent in 2001-12 respectively. The other/unspecified group of countries registered a marginal increase in the share in total exports of India over the same period of study. The annual growth rate of 15.8 per cent of total exports of India is considered as the benchmark for the period of 1994-95 to 2011-12. The OPEC countries, developing countries and others/unspecified countries registered a higher growth rate than the benchmark growth rate and the remaining groups like OECD countries and Eastern Europe countries grew at a lower growth rate than the benchmark growth rate over the same period of time. It is clear from the analysis that the direction of exports of India over the period of study saw a change in favour of OPEC countries and developing countries. The traditional trade partners of India lost the share in exports from India over the period and new trends in direction of Indian exports emerged.

Table 4.11: Growth and Direction of Exports of India, 1994-1995 to 2011-2012

Year	OECD Countries	OPEC	Eastern Europe	Developing Countries	Others/ Unspecified	Total Trade
1994-95	15443.8 (58.7)	2428.6 (9.2)	1057.1 (4.0)	6969.5 (26.5)	431.5 (1.6)	26330.5
1995-96	17705.1 (55.7)	3079 (9.7)	1340 (4.2)	9198.4 (28.9)	472.4 (1.5)	31794.9
1996-97	18601.4 (55.6)	3228.8 (9.6)	1098.5 (3.3)	10036.7 (30.0)	504.3 (1.5)	33469.7
1997-98	19484.9 (55.7)	3527.4 (10.1)	1283.3 (3.7)	10312.1 (29.5)	398.7 (1.1)	35006.4
1998-99	19264 (58.0)	3550.7 (10.7)	1052.9 (3.2)	9221.3 (27.8)	129.8 (0.4)	33218.7
1999-00	21106.6 (57.3)	3895.8 (10.6)	1292.9 (3.5)	10460 (28.4)	67.1 (0.2)	36822.4

Year	OECD Countries	OPEC	Eastern Europe	Developing Countries	Others/ Unspecified	Total Trade
2000-01	23473.6 (52.7)	4850 (10.9)	1317.8 (3.0)	13012.6 (29.2)	1906.3 (4.3)	44560.3
2001-02	21622.1 (49.3)	5224.5 (11.9)	1254.8 (2.9)	13535.5 (30.9)	2189.8 (5.0)	43826.7
2002-03	26382.6 (50.0)	6884.6 (13.1)	1248.1 (2.4)	17862.3 (33.9)	341.8 (0.6)	52719.4
2003-04	29629.2 (46.4)	9544.4 (14.9)	1555.4 (2.4)	22784.3 (35.7)	329.3 (0.5)	63842.6
2004-05	36494.8 (43.7)	13207.4 (15.8)	1780.2 (2.1)	31597.1 (37.8)	456.5 (0.5)	83535.9
2005-06	45836.8 (44.5)	15242.2 (14.8)	1980.4 (1.9)	39736.4 (38.5)	294.6 (0.3)	103091
2006-07	53056.9 (42.0)	20953.1 (16.6)	1554.1 (1.2)	50417.2 (39.9)	432.8 (0.3)	126414
2007-08	64272.1 (39.5)	26989.7 (16.6)	1836.7 (1.1)	69171.1 (42.5)	634.6 (0.4)	162904
2008-09	68452.3 (36.9)	38872.8 (21.0)	2012.6 (1.1)	68545.9 (37.0)	7411.4 (4.0)	185295
2009-10	64141.6 (35.9)	37648.6 (21.1)	1793.3 (1.0)	70099.8 (39.2)	5068 (2.8)	178751
2010-11	83350.7 (33.2)	53502 (21.3)	2813.5 (1.1)	96039.8 (38.2)	15430.2 (6.1)	251136
2011-12	103493 (33.8)	58070.6 (19.0)	3244.2 (1.1)	124705 (40.8)	16450.9 (5.4)	305964
TGR	11.8	22.2	5.4	18.9	21.6	15.8

Source: www.rbi.org.in Reserve Bank of India

Due to availability of abundant labour force, impressive artistic and natural resources, adequate language skills and strong historical linkages across the world, BRICS, SAARC and many developing countries of the world have the potential to become exporters of services such as, tourism, health and education, IT and software, financial and business outsourcing-related services. In this section, an attempt has been made to look at the direction of services exports of India to major countries of the world. Though the data regarding country-wise exports of services of India is not available, but some indicators of exports are being presented.

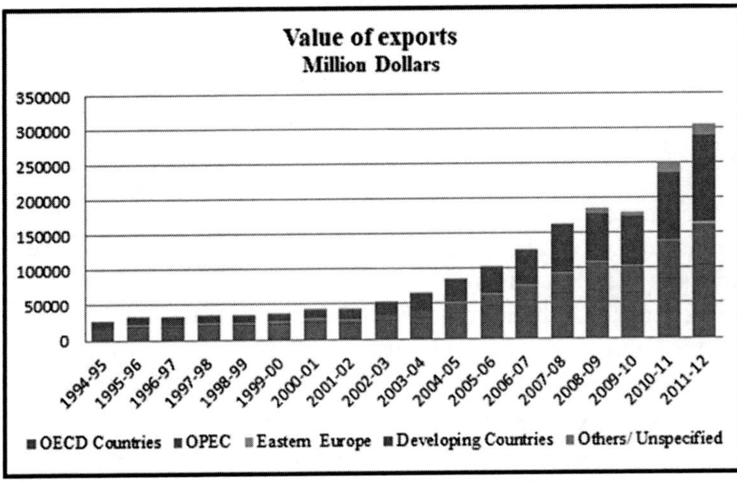

Figure 4.12: Direction of Exports of India, 1994-1995 to 2011-2012

Source: Based on Table 4.11

India contributed about 1.1 per cent (US $ 1.14 billion) in the US total imports of services during the years 2002 and 2003. During 2002, US travel imports from India consisted of US $ 726 million which constitutes about 1.2 per cent of US's total travel imports. In the European Union, during the year 2003, total imports of services share of India was 0.4 per cent (US $ 3.2 billion). During the same year, the share of India in European Union's travel services imports was about 0.5 per cent and that in transport services imports 0.5 per cent. In UK's total services imports during 2003 India contributed about 0.9 per cent. During the same year India's share in UK's imports of commercial services, travel services and transport services was about 0.8 per cent, 1.2 per cent and 1.1 per cent respectively. In case of Japan, in its total services imports during 2003 India's share was about 0.2 per cent. India's share in Japan's imports of other commercial services, travel services and transport services was 0.3 per cent, 0.3 per cent and 0.3 per cent respectively during 2003. India's exports of services direction reveals that

USA, European Union, UK and Japan are the destinations of Indian services exports and this strategic trade relationship would defiantly help India to increase exports of services in future.

To sum up, the need of international trade arises because the countries have different production capabilities and specialisations in producing different goods and services. Under the perfect competition conditions, the basic and fundamental principle of international trade should be that a country buys goods and services from the country which has the lowest prices and sell goods and services to the country which offers highest prices. Therefore, the international trade injects global competition and hence domestic industry tends to become competitive and efficient, therefore, international trade is very important and crucial for all the countries in the world. But many countries of the world reluctantly opened their economies to protect their people from harmful effects of international trade by introducing barriers and restrictions.

Analysis of international trade shows that it increased in volume, value and registered satisfactory growth mainly due to liberalisation of trade in goods and services. Region-wise analysis of world trade clearly brought out that developed economies still dominate and lead in trade in services in the world market and considered to be a challenge before the developing and transition economies. It can be concluded that the WTO and GATS agreements and provisions of trade liberalisation has helped the growth of world trade in goods as well as in services across the globe.

The study of India's exports of goods and services in total exports of India clearly shows that exports of services have been emerging future area of exports from India. It can be concluded on the basis of important indicators, viz. share of India's services exports in total exports of India, share of services exports of India in World services exports, annual percentage change of services exports of India and comparatively high growth rate of services share in India's export that the services exports seems to be the future growth engine of Indian economy.

Services exports of India, BRICS and SAARC describe the change in demand pattern of the series and an increasing trend of services exports from developing countries. Technological advancements and availability of skilled labour have led to tradability of newly emerged services which were not traded earlier and hence new areas of services exports have emerged over the period. The analysis of services exports of BRICS countries clearly indicates that India was able to increase its share of services exports over the period of study, whereas the other members of the BRICS registered a decline in their share of services exports. India is now seen as an emerging hub of services exports in the BRICS as it has the highest share of services exports in the BRICS countries. India also emerged as the leader of services exports among the SAARC countries and it is clear that trade liberalisation policies have facilitated India and helped it to fuel its growth engine in services exports and achieve this position.

The composition of services exports of India, BRICS, SAARC and world has witnessed drastic changes over the period of study. The shift was seen in the composition of services, i.e. the entry and emergence of non-traditional and newly emerging services which were not traded earlier due to technological backwardness. But with boost in new technologies, tradability of various services became possible and new areas of services were able to increase their share and positively affected the growth rate of exports of services. The latest trends of services exports indicate that the traditional services grew at lower growth rates as compared to non-traditional newly emerging services which grew at higher growth rates. Analysis of direction of exports of India over the period of study has witnessed a change in favour of OPEC countries and developing countries. The traditional trading partners of India lost the share in exports from India and new trends in direction of Indian exports emerged. The direction of India's exports of services reveals that USA, European Union, UK and Japan are the destinations of Indian services exports and this would help India to increase exports of services in future.

❐

Chapter 5

Services Exports of India: Competitiveness and Performance

5.1 Introduction

The performance and competitiveness of exports of services of any country can be measured by using various indices and indicators such as market share in overall world exports, export structure, export performance index and revealed comparative advantage index. These values of indices and indicators is determined by many factors like institutional set up, infrastructural facilities, macro-economic environment, labour market, financial market flexibility, technological changes, size of the market, trade policy and associated trade agreements. Literature has also highlighted the role of factor endowments, especially the availability of an adequate supply of relatively highly-skilled labour, suitable for the production and export of modern services, such as the adequacy of telecommunications services and extent of internet penetration and the supportive policies specific to services, such as favourable tax treatment and special economic zones to increase the performance and competitiveness of services exports (Eichengreen and Gupta, 2012). The factors that drive services growth are some of the important demand side factors which include sources of change in aggregate demand and income elasticity of demand for services. Increase in services exports along with positive shifts in propensity to consume services also tend to increase services growth and as a result services sector tends to lead the overall growth in the economy. Along with these factors one more important factor that accelerates GDP in services is high income elasticity of demand for services (Rakshit, 2007). Further, the GATS rules for liberalizing trade in services and specific commitments on market access and national treatment has raised the profile of service industries and prepared especially transition and developing economies to their potential as additional sources of revenue for national economies (Daniels, 2000). As a consequence, the economic transformation and structural changes in both developing and developed countries has paved the way for the growing contribution of the services sector in economic growth, employment, and trade (Chemsripong and Mahmood, 2008).

Exports performance and competitiveness of any country depends upon domestic resource endowment, production structure, stage of economic development, economic planning and economic policies being pursued. Recently, it has been established that the exports of services has been the dominant growth engine across the globe. Consequently, the interest to study the realized performance and competitiveness in exports of services has increased exponentially. In this chapter an attempt has been made to investigate and probe the competitiveness and performance of India's services exports with special reference to world, BRICS and major SAARC countries.[1] This chapter is organised into four sections. Introduction to the competitiveness and performance of services exports of India has been discussed in section 5.1. The overview of comparative economic and trade in services profile of India, world, BRICS and SAARC countries has been presented in section 5.2. India's services exports competitiveness and related variables have been analysed in section 5.3. In section 5.4 India's services exports performance has been discussed. The emerging issues and conclusions regarding India's services exports competitiveness and performance have been presented in the last section of the chapter.

5.2 India, World, BRICS and SAARC: General Profile and Services Trade

Before discussing and evaluating the competitiveness and performance of India's exports of services, it is of paramount importance to look at the economic and services trade profile of countries in comparison to world, BRICS and major SAARC countries. The data and information of various indicators of economic and trade profile in services of India, world, BRICS and major SAARC economies have been portrayed in Table 5.1.

The analysis for BRICS countries shows that Russia has the largest landmass in the group followed by China, Brazil, India and South Africa. But the most populous countries in this group include China with the highest population of 1,370 million followed by India with 1,267 million. The least populous country in the BRICS group was South Africa with 52.52 million people registered in 2014. In case of poverty headcount ratio South Africa registered the highest percentage of 45.5 in 2011. India also recorded a high 21.9 per cent poverty headcount ratio in the year 2013. This was followed by Russia (11.0 per cent) and Brazil (8.9 per cent) in the year 2013. The life expectancy for the year 2012 was highest for Brazil with 74 years. It was followed by China, Russia, India and South Africa with 72 years, 70 years, 66 years and 56 years respectively during the same year. The unemployment rate for the year 2013 was the highest for South Africa with 24.9 per cent. In the same year Brazil recorded 6.5 per cent unemployment rate followed by Russia, India and China with 5.5 per cent, 4.5 per cent and 4.0 per cent respectively. The human development index ranking for the BRICS countries for the year 2013 reveal that Russia with HDI ranks of 57, Brazil with 79 and China with 91 were among the high human development group. However, South Africa and India with ranks 118 and 135 respectively come under medium human development index.

Table 5.1: Economic and Services Trade Profile of BRICS and SAARC Countries

Country Profile	Area (km²)	Population (Million) 2014	Poverty Headcount ratio at national poverty lines (% of population)	Life Expectancy (years) 2012	Unemployment Rate (2013)	HDI Ranking 2013
Brazil	8,514,877	202.0	8.9 (2013)	74	6.5	79
Russia	17,098,242	141.0	11.0 (2013)	70	5.5	57
India	3,287,263	1267	21.9 (2013)	66	4.5	135
China	9,596,961	1370		72	4.0	91
South Africa	1,221,037	52.52	45.5 (2011)	56	24.9	118
Afghanistan	652,864	31.28	35.8 (2011)	61	8.2 (2011)	169
Bangladesh	147,570	158.5	31.5 (2010)	70	4.5 (2010)	142
Bhutan	38,394	7,66,000	12.0 (2012)	68	2.9	136
Maldives	298	3,52,000		78	11.7 (2010)	103
Nepal	147,181	28.12	25.2 (2010)	68	3.3	145
Pakistan	803,940	185.1	12.4 (2011)	66	6.2	146
Sri Lanka	65,610	21.33	6.7 (2013)	74	4.4	73
Economic Profile Countries	**GDP (Current US $) 2013**	**Annual GDP Growth (%) 2013**	**Gross National Income (GNI) per capita (Current US $) 2013**	**FDI Net Inflows (% of GDP) 2012**		
Brazil	2.246 trillion	2.3	11,690	3.4		
Russia	2.097 trillion	1.3	13,850	2.6		
India	1.877 trillion	4.7	1,570	1.7		
China	9.240 trillion	7.7	6,560	3.0		
South Africa	350.6 billion	1.9	7,190	1.5		
Afghanistan	20.31 billion	3.6	690	0.5		
Bangladesh	150.0 billion	6.0	1,010	1.0		
Bhutan	1.781 billion	5.6	2,330	0.9		
Maldives	2.300 billion	3.7	5,600	13.1		
Nepal	19.29 billion	3.6	730	0.5		
Pakistan	232.3 billion	3.7	1,360	0.4		
Sri Lanka	67.18 billion	7.3	3,170	1.6		

Services Trade Profile	Exports (2012)			Imports (2012)		
Countries	**Value**	**% of Total World**	**% annual Change**	**Value**	**% of Total World**	**% annual Change**
Brazil	39864	0.9	4.3	80939	1.9	6.3
Russia	59104	1.3	7.0	106313	2.5	18.9
India	146144	3.3	5.3	128837	3.0	3.3
China	191430	4.3	8.5	281204	6.6	18.1
South Africa	15148	0.3	2.2	17671	0.4	-10.1
Afghanistan	3056	0.1	-12.1	2239	0.1	73.8
Bangladesh	2642	0.1	9.1	5578	0.1	5.8
Bhutan	102	0.0	24.8	197	0.0	11.3
Maldives	2016	0.0	0.5	587	0.0	8.3
Nepal	925	0.0	7.1	896	0.0	14.6
Pakistan	6600	0.1	31.1	8417	0.2	5.7
Sri Lanka	3800	0.1	23.2	2538	0.1	-36.7

Note: 1. Figures in parenthesis are respective years

Source: 1. World Bank data, http://data.worldbank.org, 2. ILO statistics, http://www.ilo.org, 3. UNDP Human Development Indicators, http://hdrstats.undp.org

The country-wise profile of SAARC countries shows that India is the largest country in terms of land area covered and population. In case of poverty headcount the highest was recorded by Afghanistan with 35.8 per cent for the year 2011 followed by Bangladesh with 31.5 per cent for year 2010, Nepal with 25.2 per cent for year 2010 and India with 21.9 per cent for 2013. The countries which registered a relatively low percentage of poverty headcount were Pakistan with 12.4 per cent for 2011, Bhutan with 12.0 per cent for 2012 and Sri Lanka with 6.7 per cent for 2013. Life expectancy for SAARC countries during 2012 was highest for Maldives with 78 years followed by Sri Lanka and Bangladesh with 74 years and 70 years respectively. The countries which registered lower life expectancy were Bhutan, Nepal, India and Pakistan with 68 years, 68 years, 66 years and 66 years respectively. Afghanistan recorded the lowest life expectancy at 61 years during the same year. The highest unemployment rate was recorded by Maldives with 11.7 per cent in the year 2010, followed by Afghanistan with 8.2 per cent in the year 2011. The lowest unemployment rate was registered by Bhutan with 2.9 per cent in the year 2013. In case of HDI ranking, Sri Lanka with a rank 73 was only SAARC country in the high human development group. Bangladesh, Bhutan and Maldives with ranks 142, 136 and 103 respectively were in the medium human development group and Nepal, Pakistan and Afghanistan with ranks 145, 146 and 169 respectively were in the low human development group.

The economic profile of BRICS countries shows that during the year 2013 China recorded the highest level of GDP in the group with US $ 9.240 trillion, followed by Brazil, Russia and India with US $ 2.246 trillion, US $ 2.097 trillion and US $ 1.877 trillion respectively. South Africa recorded the lowest GDP of US $ 350.6 billion during the same year. The highest annual GDP growth for the year 2013 was in case of China with 7.7 per cent, followed by India, Brazil, South Africa and Russia with 4.7 per cent, 2.3 per cent, 1.9 per cent and 1.3 per cent respectively. GNI per capita for the year 2013 was highest for Russia with US $ 13,850 followed by Brazil (US $ 11,690) and lowest for India (US $ 1,570). Highest FDI net inflow in 2012 was recorded by Brazil with 3.4 per cent of the GDP followed by China with 3.0 per cent of the GDP. India and South Africa recorded the lowest net inflow of FDI with 1.7 per cent of GDP and 1.5 per cent of GDP respectively during the same year.

The analysis of economic profile of SAARC countries shows that India had the largest GDP in the year 2013 with level of US $ 1.877 trillion in the group. It was followed by Pakistan and Bangladesh with US $ 232.2 billion and US $ 150.0 billion respectively. The lowest GDP for the same year was registered by Bhutan with US $ 1.781 billion. The highest annual GDP growth for the year 2013 was registered by Sri Lanka with 7.3 per cent followed by Bangladesh, Bhutan and India with 6.0 per cent, 5.6 per cent and 4.7 per cent respectively. The lowest annual GDP growth for the same year was recorded by Afghanistan and Nepal with 3.6 per cent for both. The highest GNI per capita for 2013 was registered by Maldives with US $ 5600 followed by Sri Lanka, Bhutan, India and Pakistan with US $ 3,170, US $ 2,330, US $ 1,570 and US $ 1,360 respectively. The lowest GNI per capita for the same year was registered by Nepal and Afghanistan with US $ 730 and US $ 690 respectively. The highest 13.21 per cent of GDP net inflow of FDI was of Maldives and the lowest FDI net inflow was recorded by Pakistan with 0.4 per cent of GDP in 2013.

The analysis of services trade profile of the BRICS countries shows that China registered the highest percentage share of services exports in world with 4.3 per cent followed by India with 3.3 per cent during 2012. In case of imports also China registered the highest share of services imports in the world with 6.6 per cent again followed by India with 3.0 per cent share in the same year. The lowest share in both services exports and services imports was registered by South Africa with 0.3 per cent share in total world services exports and 0.4 per cent share in total world services imports.

In the year 2012 India registered the highest share of services exports in total world exports with 3.3 per cent and also registered highest share of services imports in total world exports with 3.0 per cent among the SAARC group of countries. The other countries of the SAARC group had a very less share in both exports and imports of services in total world services exports and imports.

Above analysis and discussion of all the three profile indicators clearly suggests that there were many similarities among India, BRICS and SAARC countries. Therefore, it is of crucial importance and viable to carry comparative competitiveness and performance analysis of services exports among India and other BRICS and major SAARC countries. In this light, an attempt has been made to investigate and probe the competitiveness and performance services exports of India during period 2000-12.

5.3 Services Exports: Competitiveness

In literature different methods have been applied to evaluate and measure the competitiveness of exports such as revealed comparative advantage index, regression analysis, observed export share index, adjusted export share index and openness factor index (Peterson and Barras, 1987). Due to some problems associated with the different measures of competitiveness to asses a country's competitiveness in international trade in services, the comprehensive analysis of competitiveness has remained lacking. In such a situation, in the present study multiple indices and indicators have been used to gauge and present a comprehensive and holistic view of India's competitiveness in international trade in services and these have been discussed in the next section.

5.3.1 *Global Competitiveness of India: Overview*

To evaluate and measure the global competitiveness of countries, the earlier index of global competitiveness based on 9 pillar approach, presently 12 pillars has been introduced and provided by World Economic Forum in 2006 (Global Competitiveness Report, 2006-07). These pillars include institutional setup, infrastructural facilities, macroeconomic environment, health and primary education facilities, higher education and training facilities, efficiency of goods market, efficiency of labour market, development of financial market, technological readiness, size of the market, complexity of business processes and innovation. Under this criterion the competitiveness has been defined as the set of institutions, policies and factors that determine the productivity levels of a country (Global Competitiveness Report, 2013-14). On the bases of these pillars the World Economic Forum rank the countries according to their position and score in the world competitiveness. In the above view, to analyse the comparative global competitiveness of India, an overview based on 12 pillars framework of world economic forum has been carried out (Global Competitiveness Report, 2007-08). The information and data with regard to India's global competitiveness has been shown in Table 5.2.

During 2008-09, India was ranked 50th out of 134 countries in composite world competitiveness index with a score of 4.33 out of seven and in 2013-14 India was ranked 60th out of 148 countries in composite world competitiveness index with a score of 4.28. This reveals that during the period 2008-09 to 2013-14, the rank position remained above the middle and the score remained almost the same.

The analysis of the various pillars shows that the score of the basic requirements remained the same at 4.23 in 2008-09 and 2013-14 and the rank of India was 80th out of 134 countries and 96th out of 148 countries respectively in 2008-09 and 2013-14. Further, under the basic requirements, the first pillar, institutions registered a score of 4.223 in 2008-09 which decreased to 3.86 in 2013-14 out of seven. The world rank of India on the basis of this pillar was 53rd in 2008-09 and 72nd in 2013-14. Second pillar, infrastructural facilities had a score of 3.38 in 2008-09 which increased slightly to 3.65 in 2013-14. The rank position of infrastructural facilities was 72nd and 85th respectively in 2008-09 and 2013-14. The third pillar of macroeconomic environment recorded the score of 4.32 in 2008-09 and it decreased to 4.10 in 2013-14. The rank position registered a difference of one rank and it was 109 in 2008-09 and 110 in 2013-14. The fourth and the last pillar under the basic requirements was health and primary education facilities which registered an increase in score from 4.99 in 2008-09 to 5.30 in 2013-14 and the rank position registered a difference of two ranks, 100th rank position in 2008-09 and 102th in 2013-14.

The second group of factors called efficiency enhancers registered a score of 4.49 in 2008-09 which decreased to 4.41 in 2013-14. The rank position of efficiency enhancers was 33rd in 2008-09 and 42nd in 2013-14. Under efficiency enhancers, the fifth pillar of higher education and training registered the score of 4.06 in 2008-09 and in 2013-14 it was 3.88 and the rank position for the fifth pillar was 63rd in 2008-09 and in 2013-14 it was 91st. The sixth pillar which was efficiency of goods market registered a score of 4.52 in 2008-09 and this score decreased to 4.18 in 2013-14 and the rank position was 47th in 2008-09 and in 2013-14 it was 85th. The seventh pillar of labour market efficiency had a score of 4.16 in 2008-09 and in 2013-14 it decreased to 4.08. The rank in case of this pillar was

89th in 2008-09 and 99th in case of 2013-14. The development of financial market, the eighth pillar registered the score of 4.98 in 2008-09 and 4.83 in 2013-14. The rank position in the case of eighth pillar was 34th in 2008-09 which improved to 19th in 2013-14. The ninth pillar of technological readiness had a score of 3.27 in 2008-09 which decreased slightly to 3.22 in 2013-14. The rank position in 2008-09 was 69th and in 2013-14 the rank position was 98th. The tenth and last pillar in the group of efficiency enhancers is size of the market which recorded an increase in its score from 5.96 in 2008-09 to 6.25 in 2013-14. The rank in case of the tenth pillar was 5th in 2008-09 which improved to 3rd in 2013-14.

Table 5.2: India's Position and Score in Services Competitiveness in World

	Position		Score (1-7)	
Competitiveness Variables/ Pillars	2013-14 (out of 148)	2008-09 (out of 134)	2013-14	2008-09
World Competitiveness Index	60	50	4.28	4.33
Basic Requirements	**96**	**80**	**4.23**	**4.23**
Pillar 1: institutions	72	53	3.86	4.23
Pillar 2: infrastructure	85	72	3.65	3.38
Pillar 3: macroeconomic environment	110	109	4.10	4.32
Pillar 4: health and primary education	102	100	5.30	4.99
Efficiency Enhancers	**42**	**33**	**4.41**	**4.49**
Pillar 5: higher education and training	91	63	3.88	4.06
Pillar 6: goods market efficiency	85	47	4.18	4.52
Pillar 7: labour market efficiency	99	89	4.08	4.16
Pillar 8: financial market development	19	34	4.83	4.98
Pillar 9: technological readiness	98	69	3.22	3.27

	Position		Score (1-7)	
Competitiveness Variables/ Pillars	**2013-14 (out of 148)**	**2008-09 (out of 134)**	**2013-14**	**2008-09**
Pillar 10: market size	3	5	6.25	5.96
Innovation and Sophistication Factors	**41**	**27**	**4.00**	**4.29**
Pillar 11: business complexity	42	27	4.38	4.85
Pillar 12: innovation	41	32	3.62	3.74

Source: World Competitiveness Reports, World Economic Forum (relevant issues).

The last set of factors called the innovation and sophistication saw a decrease in the score from 4.29 in 2008-09 to 4.00 in 2013-14. The rank in this case declined from 27th in 2008-09 to 41st in 2013-14. The eleventh pillar which is the complexity of business processes registered a decrease in the score from 4.85 in 2008-09 to 4.38 in 2013-14 and the rank position was registered at 27th in 2008-09 and 42nd in 2013-14. The 12th and the last pillar of innovation had a score of 3.74 in 2008-09 and it was 3.62 in 2013-14. The rank position in case of the 12th pillar was 32nd in 2008-09 and it was 41st in 2013-14.

The analysis of India's composite world competitiveness index shows that both the rank position and score remained unchanged. Under the basic requirements the overall rank position and score also remained the same during 2008-09 and 2013-14. However, though the score of infrastructural facilities improved but rank remained well below the middle. In case of institutions, macroeconomic environment and health and primary education pillars the scores of India almost remained the same and rank position was well below the middle level. It is clearly evident that India could not improve her position with regard to basic requirements for global competitiveness. In case of second group of pillars which contribute to efficiency enhancers it is observed that the position of India in overall efficiency enhancers remained satisfactory due to high score and high rank during the same period. The analysis of higher education and training, efficiency of goods market, labour market efficiency, development of financial markets and technological readiness represents a mixed picture. However, size of the market as an efficiency enhancer pillar improved its score and rank appreciably. The last set of pillars remained well above the middle level during 2008-09 and 2013-14. Under this the complexity of business processes and innovations suggest that these remained well above the middle level. Therefore, the analysis of various contributory pillars/factors suggests that India needs to do much more progress and to initiate policy measures on this front to compete globally.

5.3.2 *Services Exports: Observed Exports Share (OES)*

An attempt has been made to look at the comparative average annual observed export share (AAOES) in services exports of India, Brazil, Russia, China, South Africa, Pakistan, Bangladesh and Sri Lanka in the total services exports of world in different service categories during the period 2000-12. Further, to analyse the annual growth of different services exports compound annual growth rates (CAGR) of various services have been worked out. The information of observed export shares and CAGR has been presented in Table 5.3 and the formula applied to drive annual average observed export share index is given in equation 5.1.

Annual Average Observed Export Share (AAOES) index =

$$\left[\frac{X_{Ii}}{X_{Wi}} \times 100\right] \qquad \ldots (5.1)$$

Where X_{Ii} = India's services exports of service i

X_{Wi} = World's services exports of service i

Average annual observed export share represents (Peterson and Barras, 1987) the share of India's exports of services in the world's exports of services (e.g. share of India's travel services exports in world's overall travel exports).

The analysis based on annual average observed exports share index reveal that China's share was highest (3.44 per cent) followed by India (2.43 per cent), Russia (1.40 per cent), Brazil (0.73 per cent) and South Africa (0.37 per cent) in total world services exports during the period 2000-12. The share of Pakistan, Bangladesh and Sri Lanka was very low in total services exports of world during the same period.

The analysis shows that though during the period of study the annual average observed export share of China in total services exports was more than India, but the CAGR suggests that India has recorded a growth of about 23 per cent which was higher than China and all other BRICS and SAARC countries for the period 2000-12. Therefore, the indices of AAOESI suggest that India has competitiveness edge in total services exports as compared to other BRICS and SAARC countries.

The analysis of different services shows that in the transportation exports, China was the leader with AAOES level of 3.37 per cent followed by Russia (1.70 per cent), India (1.33 per cent), Brazil (0.56 per cent) and South Africa (0.23 per cent) during the period 2000-12. The share of Pakistan, Bangladesh and Sri Lanka was very low in total transportation exports of world. It also shows that China's CAGR was also the highest at 23.09 per cent followed by India with 22.42 per cent. Even though Russia's annual average observed export share was higher than India but India grew at a higher CAGR. It is clear from the analysis that though India did not have competitiveness edge, but it was not much behind the competitors in case of transportation exports during the period 2000-12.

In case of travel exports, China's AAOES was again the highest (4.26 per cent) followed by India (1.21 per cent), Russia (0.97 per cent), South Africa (0.90 per cent) and Brazil (0.55 per cent) during the period 2000-12. The share of Pakistan, Bangladesh and Sri Lanka was found to be very low. India grew at highest CAGR of 17.28 per cent during the same period. Hence, it is clear from the analysis that even though China's AAOES in total travel exports was the highest but India's growth was the highest for the period of study. Therefore, the indices namely AAOES shows that India has competitiveness edge in travel services exports.

Table 5.3: Comparative Annual Average Observed Export Share (AAOES) Index and Growth of Services Exports of India, BRICS and Major SAARC Countries, 2000-2012

Country → Service Code ↓	India	Brazil	Russia	China	South Africa	Pakistan	Bangladesh	Sri Lanka
TS	2.43 (22.69)	0.73 (15.07)	1.10 (17.03)	3.44 (18.04)	0.37 (10.46)	0.13 (12.44)	0.05 (11.97)	0.06 (9.63)
01	1.33 (22.42)	0.56 (14.11)	1.70 (14.24)	3.37 (23.09)	0.23 (3.77)	0.18 (5.83)	0.02 (11.75)	0.13 (11.99)
02	1.21 (17.28)	0.55 (13.07)	0.97 (11.51)	4.26 (10.78)	0.90 (11.87)	0.03 (14.19)	0.01 (5.44)	0.06 (8.97)
07	2.15 (8.59)	0.41 (12.20)	1.31 (14.62)	1.43 (11.03)	0.25 (9.46)	0.31 (0.17)	0.18 (30.07)	0.09 (7.29)
06	0.78 (14.54)	0.05 (-2.10)	3.70 (25.99)	8.33 (33.72)	0.06 (15.27)	0.03 (9.42)	0.02 (19.34)	0.04 (2.95)
16	1.73 (22.19)	0.52 (11.68)	0.44 (19.89)	1.62 (31.39)	0.29 (10.68)	0.05 (18.24)	0.01 (13.08)	0.13 (1.13)
13	1.24 (35.10)	0.53 (22.15)	0.32 (27.21)	0.21 (30.42)	0.28 (14.28)	0.02 (17.73)	0.01 (15.25)	–
10	16.58 (23.70)	0.11 (27.45)	0.61 (34.79)	3.40 (37.65)	0.12 (21.61)	0.08 (28.39)	0.02 (33.80)	0.12 (23.72)
14	0.07 (20.59)	0.15 (18.18)	0.17 (18.62)	0.21 (23.90)	0.02 (8.46)	0.01 (3.83)		–
15	3.50 (14.56)	1.44 (16.59)	1.12 (24.70)	4.62 (20.53)	0.12 (9.62)	0.06 (15.97)	0.04 (16.29)	0.02 (-2.43)
18	1.34 (27.60)	0.25 (0.38)	1.09 (21.07)	0.49 (22.15)	0.29 (3.33)	0.01	0.01 (0.52)	–
21	0.73 (0.81)	2.14 (10.37)	0.64 (17.67)	1.04 (10.56)	0.50 (11.78)	2.68 (24.19)	1.48 (8.59)	0.03 (0.25)

Note: 1. Figures in parenthesis are compounded annual growth rates, 2. TS - Total Service, 01 - Transport, 02 - Travel, 07 - Communication, 06 - Construction, 16 - Insurance, 13 - Financial services, 10 - Computer and Information, 14 - Royalties and License Fees, 15 - Other Business services, 18 - Personal, Cultural and Recreational services, 21 - Government services

Source: Calculated from UNCTADSTAT, United Nations Conference on Trade and Development Statistics, 2014

In case of communication services exports, India had the highest AAOES of 2.15 per cent, followed by China (1.43 per cent) and Russia (1.31 per cent) share in total world communication exports. The share of Brazil, South Africa, Pakistan, Bangladesh and Sri Lanka in total communication exports was very low. But, India lagged behind with 8.59 per cent CAGR as compared to the highest 14.62 per cent of Russia. The analysis of AAOES and CAGR suggests that India had competitiveness capacity in communication exports for the period of the study.

In case of construction services exports China was a clear leader with the highest AAOES of 8.33 per cent and also the highest CAGR of 33.72 per cent. It was followed by Russia with second highest AAOES of 3.70 per cent and also the second highest CAGR of 25.99 per cent. India followed Russia with 0.78 per cent AAOES and a CAGR of 14.54 per cent. India was followed by South Africa with 0.06 per cent AAOES and a CAGR of 15.27 per cent which was a little higher than India. The other countries Brazil, Pakistan, Bangladesh and Sri Lanka have a very low share in total world construction exports. Therefore, the AAOES and CAGR clearly suggest that China has competitiveness edge in construction services exports and India lagged far behind in this category.

In case of insurance services exports India had the highest AAOES of 1.73 per cent followed by China (1.62 per cent), Brazil (0.52 per cent), Russia (0.44 per cent) and South Africa (0.29 per cent). Pakistan, Bangladesh and Sri Lanka have a very low AAOES in insurance services. China has the highest CAGR of 31.39 per cent followed by India (22.19 per cent) and Russia (19.89 per cent) in insurance services exports. Again, the AAOES and CAGR indices brought out that India has a competitiveness edge in insurance services exports.

In case of financial services India had the highest AAOES of 1.24 per cent followed by Brazil (0.53 per cent), Russia (0.32 per cent), South Africa (0.28 per cent) and China (0.21 per cent). Pakistan, Bangladesh and Sri Lanka have a very low share. India also registered the highest CAGR of 35.10 per cent followed by China (30.42 per cent), Russia (27.21 per cent) and

Brazil (22.15 per cent). This suggests that AAOES and CAGR clearly show that India has a competitiveness power in financial services exports.

In case of computer and information services exports, India has the highest AAOES of 16.58 per cent followed by China (3.40 per cent) and Russia (0.61 per cent). Other countries Brazil, South Africa, Pakistan, Bangladesh and Sri Lanka have a very low share. China registered the highest CAGR of 37.65 per cent followed by Russia (34.79 per cent) and India (23.70 per cent). Though the countries like Brazil, South Africa, Pakistan, Bangladesh and Sri Lanka had a very low AAOES in computer and information services but they registered high CAGR of 27.45 per cent, 21.61 per cent, 28.39 per cent, 33.80 per cent and 23.72 per cent respectively. Thus, India has a competitiveness edge in computer and information services exports.

In case of royalties and license fees services exports China has the highest AAOES of 0.21 per cent and also the highest CAGR of 23.90 per cent during 2000-12. In AAOES, China was followed by Russia (0.17 per cent) and Brazil (0.15 per cent). The rest of the countries India, South Africa, and Pakistan registered very low AAOES. In case of CAGR, China was followed by India (20.59 per cent), Russia (18.62 per cent) and Brazil (18.18 per cent). The analysis of AAOES and CAGR for loyalties and license fees services exports indicate that India did not have competitiveness.

In case of other business services exports China had the highest AAOES of 4.62 per cent followed by India (3.50 per cent), Brazil (1.44 per cent) and Russia (1.12 per cent) during 2000-12. The share of South Africa, Pakistan, Bangladesh and Sri Lanka was very low and the CAGR of 24.70 per cent was highest of Russia followed by China (20.53 per cent), Brazil (16.59 per cent) and India (14.56 per cent) during 2000-12. Therefore, the analysis in this regard indicates that India's position is second only to China and it has competitiveness edge in case of other business services.

The study of personal, cultural and recreational services shows that India has the highest AAOES of 1.34 per cent and the highest CAGR of 27.60 per cent during 2000-12. Russia with AAOES of 1.09 per cent, China (0.49 per cent), South Africa (0.29 per cent) and Brazil (0.25 per cent) followed India. The CAGR of China was second highest (22.15 per cent), followed by Russia (21.07 per cent). The AAOES and CAGR of the rest of countries Brazil, South Africa, Pakistan and Bangladesh were very low. Therefore, India had competitiveness edge in case of personal, cultural and recreational services category.

In case of government services exports Pakistan has the highest AAOES of 2.68 per cent and the highest CAGR of 24.19 per cent among the group of countries being analysed. It was followed by Brazil (2.14 per cent), Bangladesh (1.48 per cent) and China (1.04 per cent). The rest of the countries like India, Russia, South Africa and Sri Lanka have a very low AAOES. The second highest CAGR was recorded by Russia (17.67 per cent), South Africa (11.78 per cent), China (10.56 per cent) and Brazil (10.37 per cent). Therefore, the AAOES indices clearly indicates that India has a very low share in government services and did not have competitiveness edge.

The information of OES of India's various services exports to world during 2000-12 has been depicted in Table 5.4.

The data shows that the OES of total services exports of India to world has increased from 1.10 per cent in 2000 to 3.27 per cent in 2012. Similarly, the OES of transport services exports increased from 0.57 per cent to 1.97 per cent, travel services exports from 0.73 per cent to 1.63 per cent, insurance services exports from 0.93 per cent to 2.17 per cent, financial services exports from 0.28 per cent to 1.66 per cent, computer and information services from 8.87 per cent to 18.05 per cent, other business services from 2.34 to 4.10 per cent and personal, cultural and recreational services exports from 0.20 per cent to 1.94 per cent during the same period. However, the OES of communications services exports declined from 1.75 per cent to 1.48 per cent, services exports of construction from 1.66 per cent to 0.86 per cent and government services from 2.13 per cent to 0.64 per cent during the study period. The OES of royalties and license fee exports almost remained the same over the period of study.

Table 5.4: Observed Exports Share (OES) of India in Services Exports of World, 2000-2012

Service Code → ↓ Year	TS	01	02	07	06	16	13	10	14	15	18	21
2000	1.10	0.57	0.73	1.75	1.66	0.93	0.28	8.87	0.09	–	–	2.13
2001	1.14	0.60	0.68	3.04	0.21	0.95	0.33	11.19	0.04	–	–	1.66
2002	1.19	0.70	0.64	2.08	0.65	0.75	0.60	11.14	0.02	–	–	0.97
2003	1.26	0.75	0.82	2.15	0.70	0.75	0.31	11.42	0.02	–	–	0.59
2004	1.66	0.87	0.95	2.03	1.11	1.49	0.22	12.99	0.04	2.34	0.20	0.67
2005	2.04	1.01	1.07	2.64	0.62	1.90	0.63	15.49	0.13	3.05	0.48	0.58
2006	2.40	1.19	1.13	3.06	0.90	1.79	1.05	17.02	0.04	3.63	1.29	0.43
2007	2.49	1.18	1.22	2.83	0.87	1.96	1.14	17.60	0.08	3.64	1.90	0.46
2008	2.74	1.30	1.23	2.54	0.75	1.87	1.44	18.38	0.06	3.96	2.41	0.56
2009	2.60	1.58	1.27	2.09	0.74	1.58	1.38	17.02	0.08	3.04	1.55	0.61
2010	3.00	1.64	1.52	1.59	0.53	1.84	2.07	18.24	0.05	3.51	0.99	0.71
2011	3.17	2.01	1.66	1.56	0.79	2.45	1.97	18.22	0.10	3.45	0.89	0.77
2012	3.27	1.97	1.63	1.48	0.86	2.17	1.66	18.05	0.11	4.10	1.94	0.64
AAOES	2.43	1.33	1.21	2.15	0.78	1.73	1.24	16.58	0.07	3.50	1.34	0.73

Note: 1. TS - Total Service, 01 - Transport, 02 - Travel, 07 - Communication, 06 - Construction, 16 - Insurance, 13 - Financial services, 10 - Computer and Information, 14 - Royalties and License Fees, 15 - Other Business services, 18 - Personal, Cultural and Recreational services, 21 - Government services

Source: Calculated from UNCTADSTAT, United Nations Conference on Trade and Development Statistics, 2014

5.3.3 *Services Exports: Adjusted Exports Share (AES)*

Due to the limitation of OES that if a relatively large economy in terms of its GDP may have large export share mainly owing to size does not represent accurately country's competitiveness situation (Kuźnar, 2011). Therefore, to overcome this problem, in the present study another index i.e. adjusted export share (AES) has been applied (Peterson and Barras, 1987). For the purpose, the following equation number 5.2 has been used and the results of the same have been presented in Table 5.5.

$$\text{Adjusted Export Share (AES) index} = \frac{X_{Ii}/X_{ITS}}{X_{Wi}/X_{WTS}} \times 100 \qquad \dots (5.2)$$

Where; X_{Ii} = India's exports of service i

X_{ITS} = India's total services exports

X_{Wi} = World's exports of service i

X_{WTS} = World's total services exports

(a) The numerator in equation 5.2 represents the degree of export concentration of India say for travel services, i.e. share of India's travel exports in total services exports of India.

(b) The denominator shows the average degree of export concentration for world's travel services, i.e. sum of share of travel exports of all countries (i.e. total travel exports of the world).

The analysis of average adjusted exports share of India reveals that its services exports concentration has been in the computer and information services exports with index value of 681.35 and other business services with index value of 129.78. Other services categories registered very low AAES as compared to these two services and the lowest value was recorded for royalties and license fees services. Therefore, it is clear that India has specialisation and competitiveness in computer and information services and other business services over the period of study.

India's comparison with BRICS and SAARC countries reveal that in transport services, Sri Lanka has a clear specialisation

Table 5.5: Comparative Annual Average Adjusted Export Share (AAAES) Index of Services Exports of India, BRICS and Major SAARC Countries, 2000-2012

Country → Service Code ↓	India	Brazil	Russia	China	South Africa	Pakistan	Bangladesh	Sri Lanka
01	54.56	76.08	153.78	98.03	63.91	139.44	41.30	206.18
02	49.84	74.80	87.91	123.75	244.94	22.75	17.52	95.34
07	88.37	55.73	118.93	41.58	67.74	242.09	339.57	145.11
06	32.04	6.29	335.12	242.04	14.70	22.67	30.08	73.85
16	71.26	70.70	39.83	46.95	79.86	41.60	19.80	210.87
13	50.89	72.02	29.13	6.08	74.00	16.90	25.60	0.00
10	681.35	14.77	54.94	98.86	30.67	63.66	34.94	191.48
14	3.00	20.25	15.59	6.09	6.78	6.30	0.16	0.00
15	129.78	234.23	121.04	159.26	39.83	53.95	92.69	48.30
18	49.72	42.39	114.60	17.74	91.87	6.72	13.55	0.00
21	30.12	292.51	54.38	30.26	135.41	2110.70	2789.17	57.96

Note: 1. TS - Total Service, 01 - Transport, 02 - Travel, 07 - Communication, 06 - Construction, 16 - Insurance, 13 - Financial services, 10 - Computer and Information, 14 - Royalties and License Fees, 15 - Other Business services, 18 - Personal, Cultural and Recreational services, 21 - Government services

Source: Calculated from UNCTADSTAT, United Nations Conference on Trade and Development Statistics, 2014

and competitiveness with index of 206.18, followed by Russia (153.78) and Pakistan (139.44). India recorded the second lowest index of 54.56. For the travel services, South Africa registered the highest value of 244.94 followed by China with 123.75. And, India again recorded the second lowest value of 49.84 among the BRICS and SAARC countries. Therefore, in travel services South Africa has specialisation and competitiveness and in communication services Bangladesh has specialisation and competitiveness with the highest value of 339.57. It was followed by Pakistan with a value of 242.09, Sri Lanka (145.00) and Russia (118.93). For construction services Russia registered the highest value of 335.12 followed by China

(242.04). Other countries of the BRICS and SAARC have recorded very less values for construction services. Therefore, Russia has specialisation and competitiveness in construction services. In case of insurance services Sri Lanka had a clear specialisation and competitiveness with a value of 210.87. The rest of the BRICS and SAARC countries have registered very low values of the indices. For financial services, South Africa registered the highest value of 74.00 followed by Brazil (72.02) and India (50.89). Therefore, in financial services South Africa had specialisation and competitiveness.

The analysis of computer and information services reveals that India had a clear specialisation and competitiveness with an index of 681.35 and followed by Sri Lanka (191.48). Rest of the countries of the BRICS and SAARC have registered very low values of AES index. All the countries of BRICS and SAARC registered low values of the indices for royalties and license fees services. Among all the countries, Brazil had the highest value of 20.25, followed by Russia (15.59). India had the third lowest value of 3.00 and hence it did not have specialisation and competitiveness in royalties and license fees services. Brazil registered specialisation and competitiveness in this category of services. For other business services Brazil had highest value of 234.23, followed by China (159.26), India (129.78) and Russia (121.04). Among the BRICS and SAARC group of countries Brazil had specialisation and competitiveness in other business services. India also showed specialisation and competitiveness edge in the other business services. For personal, cultural and recreational services Russia had specialisation and competitiveness with a value of 114.60. Russia was followed by South Africa with a value of 91.87 and India with a value of 49.72. The other countries of the BRICS and SAARC recorded low values of the indices. In case of government services Bangladesh recorded the highest value of 2789.17, followed by Pakistan (2110.70). Bangladesh has specialisation and competitiveness in government services closely followed by Pakistan. And India registered the lowest index of 30.12 among the BRICS and SAARC countries.

Table 5.6: Adjusted Export Share (AES) Index of Services Exports of India, 2000-2012

Service Code → Years ↓	01	02	07	06	16	13	10	14	15	18	21
2000	52.12	66.19	159.30	151.63	84.60	25.80	808.88	8.24	–	–	194.58
2001	53.17	60.20	267.17	18.08	83.13	28.78	984.29	3.60	–	–	146.16
2002	58.49	53.42	174.65	54.90	62.76	50.21	934.64	1.70	–	–	81.16
2003	59.83	65.02	170.75	55.29	59.68	24.23	906.21	1.64	–	–	47.20
2004	52.39	57.09	122.25	66.91	89.55	13.37	781.20	2.25	140.75	12.11	40.54
2005	49.52	52.21	129.15	30.24	93.32	31.01	758.70	6.32	149.21	23.36	28.17
2006	49.61	47.30	127.58	37.44	74.64	43.65	709.97	1.46	151.58	53.74	18.06
2007	47.36	49.18	113.52	34.94	78.80	45.64	706.62	3.21	146.03	76.31	18.48
2008	47.47	44.90	92.72	27.41	68.35	52.53	671.74	2.37	144.91	88.21	20.41

Service Code → Years ↓	01	02	07	06	16	13	10	14	15	18	21
2009	60.89	48.81	80.30	28.43	60.57	52.85	653.98	3.12	116.74	59.70	23.26
2010	54.63	50.73	53.04	17.63	61.35	68.90	607.62	1.66	116.89	33.00	23.56
2011	63.31	52.43	49.20	24.78	77.34	62.15	574.33	3.29	108.61	28.15	24.12
2012	60.24	49.82	45.36	26.38	66.36	50.96	552.56	3.35	125.45	59.49	19.73

Note: 1. TS - Total Service, 01 - Transport, 02 - Travel, 07 - Communication, 06 - Construction, 16 - Insurance, 13 - Financial services, 10 - Computer and Information, 14 - Royalties and License Fees, 15 - Other Business services, 18 - Personal, Cultural and Recreational services, 21 - Government services

Source: Calculated from UNCTADSTAT, United Nations Conference on Trade and Development Statistics, 2014

The information of adjusted export share of India for different services during 2000-12 has been presented in Table 5.6. The analysis of AES index of services exports of India reveal that computer and information services, government services, communication services and construction services exports have highest concentration, which means that these services were competitive and India had specialisation in these service categories for the year 2000. In the year 2012 computer and information services and other business services have the highest concentration of exports and become competitive. The AES index of transport services ranges between 52.12 to 63.31, travel services between 44.90 to 66.19, communication services between 45.36 to 277.17, construction services between 17.63 to 151.63, insurance services between 60.57 to 93.32, financial services between 24.23 to 68.90, computer and information services between 552.56 to 984.29, royalties and license fees services between 1.46 to 8.24, other business services between 108.61 to 149.21, personal, cultural and recreational services between 12.11 to 88.21 and government services between 18.06 to 194.58. This presents a mixed scenario as far as AES index is concerned because in case of services such as transport, travel, insurance, financial and royalties and license fees India did not registered specialisation and competitiveness. However, for some services like computer and information and other business services India recorded specialisation and competitiveness. Further, in case of construction services and government services as the value for AES decreased, India lost its specialisation and competitiveness.

5.3.4 *Services Exports: Openness Factor (OF)*

Due to the limitations of OES and AES that if a relatively large economy in terms of its GDP may have large export share mainly owing to size and relatively does not represent accurately country's competeviness place (Kuznar, 2011). Therefore, to overcome this problem, in the present study another index called Openness Factor (OF), which demonstrates a country's dependency on trade of a particular product, has been applied (Peterson and Barras, 1987). For the purpose, the following equation number 5.3 has been used and the results of the same have been presented in Table 5.7.

$$\text{Openness Factor (OF) Index} = \frac{X_{IS} + M_{IS}}{GDP_I} \times 100 \qquad \text{...(5.3)}$$

Where X_{IS} = India's services exports
M_{IS} = India's services imports
GDP_I = India's GDP

Openness Factor (OF) index of India during the period 2000-12 reveals that the dependency on total services trade in services as percentage of GDP has increased over the period of study, because the OF index for total services trade of India has almost doubled from 7.53 per cent in 2000 to 14.79 per cent in 2012 of the GDP. For the transportation services, OF index has increased from 2.24 per cent to 4.19 per cent in 2012. In case of travel services the OF index increased from 1.29 per cent in 2000 to 1.63 per cent in 2012. The dependency of India on communication services was very low in the year 2000 with OF index equivalent to 0.15 per cent. The OF index for communication services has increased to 0.34 per cent in 2002 from 0.15 per cent in 2000 and declined to 0.14 per cent in 2012. Similarly, the OF index remained unchanged in case of construction services as the value was recorded at 0.11 per cent in 2000 and 0.13 per cent in 2012. Insurance services registered a minor increase in OF index from 0.22 per cent in 2000 to 0.47 per cent in 2012. Therefore, it can be said that India's dependency on insurance services increased slightly over the period of the study. Financial services recorded OF index of 0.33 per cent in the year 2000 and in 2012 the value of index increased to 2.69 per cent. The dependency of India on its financial services has definitely increased, but this increase was slow up to 2011 with OF index of 0.77 per cent and a sudden increase has been registered in the value of index during 2012 at 2.69 per cent. Dependency of India on computer and information services registered a steady increase in OF index 0.97 per cent in 2000 to 2.67 per cent in 2012. The indices registered a decrease in 2009 with 2.53 per cent from 2008 with 3.24 per cent. But after 2009 it has started to recover and overall dependency over the period of study recorded an increase. The dependency of India on royalties and license fees services

Table 5.7: Openness Factor (OF) Index of India's Different Services, 2000-2012

Service Code → Years ↓	TS	01	02	07	06	16	13	10	14	15	18	21
2000	7.53	2.24	1.29	0.15	0.13	0.22	0.33	0.97	0.08	-	-	0.20
2001	7.58	2.14	1.26	0.28	0.11	0.22	0.42	1.39	0.07	-	-	0.17
2002	7.73	2.10	1.16	0.34	0.16	0.23	0.39	1.43	0.07	-	-	0.12
2003	7.89	1.99	1.30	0.26	0.24	0.25	0.14	1.50	0.09	-	-	0.08
2004	10.24	2.44	1.52	0.23	0.19	0.36	0.16	1.81	0.09	3.33	0.01	0.10
2005	11.97	3.17	1.64	0.24	0.11	0.39	0.24	2.08	0.11	3.87	0.03	0.10
2006	13.53	3.42	1.63	0.29	0.15	0.40	0.45	2.46	0.10	4.52	0.04	0.08
2007	12.73	3.22	1.53	0.26	0.12	0.38	0.53	2.51	0.11	3.97	0.05	0.06
2008	15.97	4.43	1.75	0.29	0.13	0.48	0.64	3.24	0.14	4.72	0.08	0.07

Service Code → Years ↓	TS	01	02	07	06	16	13	10	14	15	18	21
2009	12.65	3.40	1.50	0.23	0.14	0.41	0.54	2.53	0.15	3.24	0.05	0.08
2010	13.54	3.49	1.46	0.16	0.09	0.40	0.74	2.43	0.15	3.51	0.05	0.07
2011	14.01	4.02	1.67	0.16	0.10	0.47	0.77	2.52	0.17	3.41	0.04	0.08
2012	14.79	4.19	1.63	0.14	0.11	0.47	2.69	2.67	0.23	4.19	0.07	0.06

Note: 1. Figures in parenthesis are compounded annual growth rates 2. TS- Total Service, 01- Transport, 02- Travel, 07- Communication, 06- Construction, 16- Insurance, 13- Financial services, 10- Computer and Information, 14- Royalties and License Fees, 15- Other Business services, 18- Personal, Cultural and Recreational services, 21- Government services

Source: Calculated from UNCTADSTAT, United Nations Conference on Trade and Development Statistics, 2014

registered a marginal increase from 0.08 per cent in 2000 to 0.23 per cent in 2012. Other business services recorded OF indices of 3.33 per cent in the year 2004 which saw decrease in 2007 (3.97 per cent) from 2006 (4.52 per cent) and in 2009 (3.24 per cent) from 2008 (4.72 per cent). But during the overall period of 2004-2012 the dependency on other business services increased. The dependency of India on personal, cultural and recreational services was very low with OF index value of 0.01 per cent in 2004. The dependency increased slightly to 0.07 per cent in 2012 and still remains very low. In case of government services the dependency of India on government services decreased from 0.20 per cent in 2000 to 0.06 per cent in 2012.

5.3.5 *Services Exports: Revealed Comparative Advantage (RCA)*

In this part of the present study a well recognized and used, Revealed Comparative Advantage (RCA) or Balassa's Index (Balassa, 1965 and 1977), has been applied to analyse the comparative advantage of Indian services exports with comparison to BRICS and major SAARC countries, Pakistan, Bangladesh and Sri Lanka. Though there are many techniques and methods to look at the revealed comparative export advantage, but the purpose to adopt RCA was that it offers a practical way of analyzing any country's comparative advantage export performance on the basis of realised exports (Islam and Siddique, 2014). For the purpose, the following equation number 5.4 has been used and the results of the same have been presented in Table 5.8.

Revealed Comparative Advantage (RCA) index

$$= \frac{X_{Ii} / X_{ITS}}{X_{Ri} / X_{RTS}} \quad \text{... (5.4)}$$

Where X_{Ii} = India's services exports of service i

X_{ITS} = India's total services exports

X_{Ri} = Rival country's services exports of i

X_{RTS} = Rival country's total services exports

Further, the value of RCA index ranges between zero and positive infinity and an RCA index of equal and greater than one demonstrate that the country has revealed comparative advantage, in other words, the country is relatively specialised in producing and exporting that service/product under consideration. An RCA closer to zero demonstrates that the country has a lower revealed comparative advantage and is not specialized in the service/product line (Balassa, 1965; Krugell and Matthee, 2009). The advantage of RCA index is that it reflects the intrinsic advantage of a particular export commodity and is consistent with changes in an economy's relative factor endowment and productivity and the disadvantages are that it cannot detect the source of comparative advantage or disadvantage (Islam and Siddique, 2014).

Table 5.8: Revealed Comparative Advantage (RCA) Index of India for Different Services, 2000-2012

Service Code	Brazil	Russia	China	South Africa	Pakistan	Bangladesh	Sri Lanka
01	0.72	0.35	0.56	0.85	0.39	1.32	0.26
02	0.67	0.57	0.40	0.20	2.19	2.84	0.52
07	1.59	0.74	2.13	1.30	0.37	0.26	0.61
06	5.09	0.10	0.13	2.09	1.24	1.07	0.42
16	1.01	1.79	1.52	0.89	1.71	3.60	0.34
13	0.71	1.75	8.37	0.66	3.01	1.99	–
10	46.13	12.40	6.89	21.32	10.70	19.50	3.42
14	0.15	0.19	0.49	0.44	0.46	18.91	–
15	0.67	1.30	0.99	3.94	2.91	1.69	3.25
18	1.42	0.50	3.39	0.63	7.84	4.21	–
21	0.10	0.53	0.99	0.22	0.01	0.01	0.52

Note: 1. 01 - Transport, 02 - Travel, 07 - Communication, 06 - Construction, 16 - Insurance, 13 - Financial services, 10 - Computer and Information, 14 - Royalties and License Fees, 15 - Other Business services, 18 - Personal, Cultural and Recreational services, 21 - Government services

Source: Calculated from UNCTADSTAT, United Nations Conference on Trade and Development Statistics, 2014

The analysis of average RCA in case of exports of transportation services in the world transportation services market reveal that India has revealed comparative advantage over Bangladesh for the period 2000-12. For rest of the BRICS and SAARC countries the value of revealed comparative advantage index was less than unity and hence India did not have revealed comparative advantage over them. In case of travel services India has revealed comparative advantage over Pakistan and Bangladesh and for rest of the countries India did not have revealed comparative advantage over its competitors. For the period 2000-12 for communication services India has revealed comparative advantage over its competitors like Brazil, China and South Africa and for the rest of the competitors the value of revealed comparative advantage index was less than unity and hence India did not have revealed comparative advantage. Analysis of exports of construction services in the world construction services market reveal that India has revealed comparative advantage over Brazil, South Africa, Pakistan and Bangladesh for the period 2000-12. In case of Russia, China and Sri Lanka the revealed comparative advantage index value was less than unity and hence India did not have revealed comparative advantage over these countries. For insurance services India had RCA over its competitors like Brazil, Russia, China, Pakistan and Bangladesh, but for South Africa and Sri Lanka the RCA index value was less than unity and hence India did not have RCA over these countries for the period 2000-12. In case of financial services India had RCA over its competitors like Russia, China, Pakistan and Bangladesh, but no RCA for Brazil and South Africa as the value of RCA index was less than unity on an average during the period 2000-12. In case of computer and information services, India has RCA over all its competitors from BRICS and SAARC countries during the period 2000-12. In case of royalties and license fees services India had RCA over Bangladesh only. For rest of the countries like Brazil, Russia, China, South Africa and Pakistan, India did not have RCA over these countries. For other business services India have RCA over Russia, South Africa, Pakistan, Bangladesh and Sri Lanka for the period 2000-12. For rest of the countries like Brazil and China India did not have RCA over these countries. For personal, cultural and recreational services India have RCA over its competitors like Brazil, China, Pakistan and Bangladesh. For rest of the countries like Russia and South Africa India did not have RCA for personal, cultural and recreational services for the period 2000-12. For government services India did not have RCA over its competitors for the period 2000-12.

5.4 Services Exports: Performance

Comparative Export Performance (CEP) index has been used to measure the competitiveness in exports of services (Serin and Civan, 2008). It is a slightly modified version of the Balassa's index and it focuses on measuring the export specialisation of a country for particular product groups. An index value of CEPI (of India) greater than the index value of any other country reveals relative comparative advantage and export performance of India against that country (Mzumara, et al., 2012). Here, to calculate the CEP index, the equation 5.5 has been used and results of the same have presented in Tables 5.9 and 5.10.

$$\text{Comparative Export Performance (CEP) index} = \frac{X_{Ii}/X_{IT}}{X_{Wi}/X_{WT}} \quad \dots (5.5)$$

Where; X_{Ii} = India's services exports of service i

X_{IT} = India's total exports

X_{Wi} = Total world's services exports of service i

X_{WT} = Total world's exports

The analysis of comparative export performance index of India reveals that the CEP index value for transport services exports has increased from 0.76 in 2000 to 1.01 in 2012. In case of travel services exports, the value of CEP index in 2000 was 0.96 which declined to 0.83 in 2012. For communication services exports, the value of CEP index was recorded at 2.31 in 2000 which declined to a very low value of 0.76 in 2012. During the period 2000-12 construction services exports, the value of CEP index in the year 2000 was 2.20 which declined to

Table 5.9: Annual Comparative Export Performance (CEP) Index of India's Exports of Different Services, 2000-2012

Service Code → Years ↓	01	02	07	06	16	13	10	14	15	18	21
2000	0.76	0.96	2.31	2.20	1.23	0.37	11.75	0.12	–	–	2.83
2001	0.75	0.85	3.76	0.25	1.17	0.40	13.84	0.05	–	–	2.05
2002	0.79	0.72	2.36	0.74	0.85	0.68	12.65	0.02	–	–	1.10
2003	0.83	0.90	2.37	0.77	0.83	0.34	12.60	0.02	–	–	0.66
2004	0.85	0.93	1.99	1.09	1.46	0.22	12.70	0.04	2.29	0.20	0.66
2005	0.84	0.89	2.20	0.52	1.59	0.53	12.94	0.11	2.54	0.40	0.48
2006	0.91	0.87	2.35	0.69	1.38	0.80	13.09	0.03	2.79	0.99	0.33
2007	0.85	0.88	2.04	0.63	1.41	0.82	12.68	0.06	2.62	1.37	0.33
2008	0.84	0.80	1.65	0.49	1.21	0.93	11.93	0.04	2.57	1.57	0.36
2009	0.97	0.78	1.28	0.45	0.96	0.84	10.39	0.05	1.85	0.95	0.37
2010	0.89	0.83	0.87	0.29	1.00	1.13	9.94	0.03	1.91	0.54	0.39
2011	1.01	0.84	0.78	0.40	1.23	0.99	9.16	0.05	1.73	0.45	0.38
2012	1.01	0.83	0.76	0.44	1.11	0.85	9.22	0.06	2.09	0.99	0.33
Average	0.90	0.82	1.46	0.53	1.18	0.84	11.26	0.05	2.22	0.82	0.50

Note: 1. 01 - Transport, 02 - Travel, 07 - Communication, 06 - Construction, 16 - Insurance, 13 - Financial services, 10 - Computer and Information, 14 - Royalties and License Fees, 15 - Other Business services, 18 - Personal, Cultural and Recreational services, 21 - Government services

Source: Calculated from UNCTADSTAT, United Nations Conference on Trade and Development Statistics, 2014

0.44 in 2012. For insurance services exports, the value of CEP index for the year 2000 was 1.23 and this value has declined to 1.11 in the year 2012. Financial services exports has witnessed a slightly increase in the value of CEP index from 0.37 in 2000 to 0.85 in 2012. In case of computer and information services exports, the value of CEP index for the year 2000 was recorded at 11.75 which declined to 9.22 in 2012. The CEP index value for royalties and license fees services exports was recorded very low value of 0.12 in the year 2000 and throughout the period of study the value remained low and in 2012 it was 0.06. Other business services exports CEP index was 2.29 in the year 2004 and it declined to 2.09 in the year 2012. In case of personal, cultural and recreational services exports the value of CEP index was 0.20 in the year 2004 and it saw a slight increase and was recorded at 0.99 in the year 2012. For the government services the value of CEP index for the year 2000 was 2.83 and it declined over the period of study and in the year 2012 it was 0.33.

The ranking of exports of services on the basis of average CEP index during period 2000-12 suggest that computer and information services has recorded the top performance in services exports. Other business services exports, communication services exports and insurance services exports have also occupied the leading position so far the export performance of services was concerned. The exports performance of the remaining services exports except royalties and license fees services exports and government services exports remained fairly good over the period. The CEP index brought out that policy initiatives and efforts should be made for the high performance of services exports of India.

The analysis of CEP index of BRICS and major SAARC countries in comparison to India reveal that on an average in transport services exports Sri Lanka has the highest CEP index followed by Pakistan during 2000-12. However, exports performance of transportation services from India has been better than Brazil, Russia, China, South Africa and Bangladesh. For travel services the CEP index was highest for South Africa followed by Sri Lanka and again the CEP index of India was better than that of Brazil, Russia, China, Pakistan and Bangladesh.

In the case of communication services the highest CEP index has been recorded by Pakistan followed by Bangladesh, Sri Lanka and India, however the CEP index of India was higher than Brazil, Russia, China and South Africa. CEP index of construction services was highest for Russia followed by China. The CEP index of India was greater than that of Brazil, Pakistan and Bangladesh. Sri Lanka achieved the highest CEP index for insurance services exports followed by India, which was

Table 5.10: Average Annual CEP Index of Exports of Different Services of India, BRICS and SAARC Countries, 2000-2012

Service Code	India	Brazil	Russia	China	South Africa	Pakistan	Bangladesh	Sri Lanka
01	0.90	0.50	0.77	0.45	0.46	1.27	0.22	2.19
02	0.82	0.50	0.44	0.56	1.75	0.21	0.09	1.01
07	1.46	0.37	0.59	0.19	0.48	2.21	1.82	1.54
06	0.53	0.04	1.67	1.10	0.11	0.24	0.16	0.83
16	1.18	0.47	0.20	0.21	0.57	0.38	0.11	2.24
13	0.84	0.48	0.15	0.03	0.55	0.15	0.14	–
10	11.26	0.10	0.27	0.45	0.23	0.58	0.19	2.16
14	0.05	0.13	0.08	0.03	0.05	0.06	0.001	–
15	2.2	1.31	0.51	0.61	0.24	0.41	0.42	0.43
18	0.82	0.23	0.48	0.07	0.55	0.06	0.06	–
21	0.50	1.94	0.28	0.14	0.97	19.24	14.99	0.62

Note: 1. 01 - Transport, 02 - Travel, 07 - Communication, 06 - Construction, 16 - Insurance, 13 - Financial services, 10 - Computer and Information, 14 - Royalties and License Fees, 15 - Other Business services, 18 - Personal, Cultural and Recreational services, 21 - Government services

Source: Calculated from UNCTADSTAT, United Nations Conference on Trade and Development Statistics, 2014

higher than most of its competitors like Brazil, Russia, China, South Africa, Pakistan and Bangladesh. Highest CEP index for financial services exports has been recorded by India. Similarly, in case of computer and information services the highest CEP index was of India at 11.26 followed by Sri Lanka with 2.16. CEP index for royalties and license fees services was very low for all the countries and the highest was recorded for Brazil with 0.13. The export performance in other business services has been the highest of India followed by Brazil. Personal, cultural and recreational services exports also have the highest CEP index of India and Pakistan has highest CEP index in government services followed by Bangladesh.

On the basis of the analysis of CEP index of BRICS and major SAARC countries in comparison to India it can be concluded that India has comparatively better performance in many services exports especially computer and information services, other business services, communication services and insurance services. At the same time it is also clear that the exports performance of India in case of remaining services exports has been comparatively good as compared to competitors.

To sum up, the exports performance and competitiveness of any country depends upon domestic resource endowment, production structure, stage of economic development, economic planning and economic policies being pursued. Recently, it has been established that the exports of services has been the dominant growth engine and as a result of this, the interest to study the reported performance and competitiveness in exports of services has grown exponentially.

On the basis of the study of various indicators of economic and services trade profile it emerged that there were many similarities among India, BRICS and SAARC countries. Therefore, it is of crucial importance and viable to carry comparative competitiveness and performance analysis of services exports among India and other BRICS and major SAARC countries. In this light, the results, the competiveness and performance of services exports of India can be generalised.

The composite world competitiveness index shows that both the rank position and score of India remained unchanged. Under the basic requirements the overall rank position and score also remained the same during 2008-09 and 2013-14. However, though the score of infrastructural facilities improved but rank remained well below the average. In case of institutions, macroeconomic environment and health and primary education pillars the scores of India almost remained the same and rank position was well below the middle level. It is evident that India could not improve her position with regard to basic requirements for global competitiveness. In case of second group of pillars which contribute to efficiency enhancers it is observed that the position of India at overall efficiency enhancers remained satisfactory due to high score and high rank during the same period. The analysis of higher education and training, efficiency of goods market, labour market efficiency, development of financial markets and technological readiness represents a mixed picture. However, size of the market as an efficiency enhancer pillar improved its score and rank appreciably. The last set of pillars remained well above the middle level during 2008-09 and 2013-14. Under this the complexity of business processes and innovations suggest that these remained well above the middle level. Therefore, the analysis of various contributory pillars/ factors suggests that India needs to do much more progress and to initiate policy measures on this front to compete globally.

On the basis of the analysis of India's annual average observed export share and CAGR of exports of services in comparison to other BRICS and SAARC countries as well as year-wise OES of different services exports, it can be concluded that it has competitiveness in total services exports during the period of study. Further, on the same basis it clearly emerged that India has competitiveness edge in travel, insurance, financial, computer and information, personal, cultural and recreational services exports. It also emerged that India has a potential for competitiveness in transportation, communication and other business services as India was not much behind its competitors in exports of these services. However, in exports of construction, royalties and license fee and government services India was found to be behind its competitors and has not been placed in any competitive position.

Annual average adjusted export shares clearly suggests that India has specialisation and competitiveness in computer and information services and other business services in comparison to other BRICS and SAARC countries over the period of study. India's comparison with BRICS and SAARC countries on the basis of AES index reveal that in transport services it has no competitiveness and specialisation on an average. AES of India presents a mixed scenario because some services like transport services, travel services, insurance services, financial services and royalties and license fees services remained low concentrated/ competitive/specialised throughout the study period. However, some services like computer and information services and other business services remained highly concentrated/competitive/ specialised over the study period. Further, construction services and government services changed from high concentration to low concentration during the period.

From the analysis of openness factor index of India's international trade in services can be concluded that its dependency on international trade in services except government services have increased over the period of study. However, India's dependency on international trade in services in case of total services, other business services, transportation services, financial services, computer and information services and travel services have outstandingly increased during the period of study.

On the basis of Revealed Comparative Advantage (RCA) index, it can be concluded that for communication services India has revealed comparative advantage over its competitors like Brazil, China and South Africa. Also, the analysis of exports of construction services in the world construction services market reveal that India has revealed comparative advantage over Brazil, South Africa, Pakistan and Bangladesh. For insurance services India had RCA over its competitors like Brazil, Russia, China, Pakistan and Bangladesh. In case of financial services India had RCA over its competitors like Russia, China, Pakistan and Bangladesh, but no RCA for Brazil and South Africa. For computer and information services India have RCA over all its competitors of BRICS and SAARC countries on an average during the period of study. For other business services India have RCA over Russia, South Africa, Pakistan, Bangladesh and Sri Lanka over the period of study and rest of the countries like Brazil and China India did not have RCA over these countries. For personal, cultural and recreational services India have RCA over its competitors like Brazil, China, Pakistan and Bangladesh.

Average CEP index ranking during period 2000-12 suggest that computer and information services has recorded the top performance in services exports followed by other business services exports, communication services exports and insurance services exports. The CEP index brought out that policy initiatives and efforts should be made for the high performance of services exports of India. Comparative export performance index of BRICS and major SAARC countries in comparison to India suggests that India has comparative better performance in many services exports especially computer and information services, other business services, communication services and insurance services.

Analysis of important indicators of India's services exports clearly holds the first hypothesis of study that India's services exports performed comparatively well than that of other suppliers in the services world market.

Note

1. For comparative analysis major SAARC countries, India, Pakistan, Bangladesh and Sri Lanka have been selected, because these country's share in services exports of SAARC as a whole was remained over 96 per cent during 2000-12 period.

Chapter 6

Services Exports of India: Major Determinants

6.1 Introduction

International trade in services has been growing significantly across the countries over the last few years. Some of the indentified determinants of exports of services are size of the economy, labour and capital productivity, human capital development, advances in technology, trade relations and agreements, exchange rate, economic growth and institutional set up. Resource allocation, efficient management, economies of scale and efficiency of production structure has also been identified as determinants of exports of goods and services (Bhagwati, 1982). The rising level of international trade in services in general has been explained by the factors like per capita income of exporter country, size of the market, international demand of services, infrastructure development, flow of FDI, exports of goods and human capital development (Eichengreen and Gupta, 2012). The demand for services exports is also influenced by level of world income, real exchange rate, financial sector development, institutional setup and services trade barriers. Economic literature suggests that as an economy improves its growth trajectory its integration with the outer world is of obvious consequence. Besides, the share of service sector in national income improves and that of agriculture and industry declines, irrespective of the production pattern in the economy (Banga, 2005). This has been proved in the growth process of the developed countries as these countries are depending more on services so far as share in GDP is concerned. It is expected that developing economy like India which has followed a high growth path must have improved the share of services in GDP. Looking at the Indian economy data it emerged that share of services increased to the level of 60 per cent at present as compared to 43 per cent in 1991 and 51 per cent in 2001 in GDP (GoI, 2014). Therefore, it seems that India may not be exception in this context. India has adopted the liberal policy environment and deeper integration towards the rest of the world from 1991. It is to be noted that this integration is not very high so far the exports as a share of GDP are concerned. But, even then the composition of exports has changed towards service sector over the period of time. The share of services exports of India in total exports for 1995, 2001 and 2012 was 17.8 per cent, 27.9 per cent and 32.9 per cent respectively. Theoretically services are divided into two segments namely, traditional services which includes services like transportation services, travel services, personal, cultural and recreational services, etc. and non-traditional services which include computer and information services, other business services, insurance services, financial services, royalties and license fees, etc. In recent decades India has shown tremendous growth in exports of non-traditional services. Consequently, composition of exports of services tilted more towards these modern services.

Competitiveness is an important factor for export performance and its sustainability. There is a lot of competition among the newly emerged economies like Brazil, China and India to corner and capture the market provided by developed countries. Hence, it is imperative to explore the various dimensions of the services exports in detail for workable policy regime in future. It is very difficult to formulate effective policy for services and their performance without knowing the nature and under currents of service sector in general and individual services in particular. This chapter is an endeavor in that context.

In economic literature, the determinants of exports of goods have been widely probed and received vast attention but there is paucity of research studies on the determinants of international trade in services especially the modern services. In this light, the present study attempts to investigate the factors determining the services exports of India and this chapter has been organised into three sections. Introduction of the problem has been presented in section 6.1 of the chapter. Theoretical setting of the problem and modelling to empirically investigate the determinants of exports of services has been discussed in section 6.2. Detailed empirical analysis of determinants of services exports has been examined in section 6.3. Finally, the major conclusions emerged from the analysis have been discussed in the last section of the chapter.

6.2 India's Services Exports: Theoretical Setting and Modelling

The analysis of the composition, competitiveness, performance, trends and patterns of services exports in the previous chapters shows that India is doing better in exports of certain services but potential exists in many other services. Service sector also plays a facilitative role in the production of physical goods for it helps to improve, firstly, the level of economic efficiency broadly means the optimal production and distribution of scarce resources; and secondly, it improves the productivity, i.e. overall ability to produce goods and services in which it acts as measure of effectiveness. High quality of service reduces the cost of production and improves the quality of product, hence generates better competitiveness. Therefore, every economy wants to improve its service infrastructure and every economy wants to have quality service from other countries particularly the services which they are not capable to produce themselves. Every service has its own peculiarities hence its export performance depends upon variety of factors. To determine the importance of these factors for the growth in exports of services it is essential to have better service specific policies. Some determinants have been identified by studying theoretical and empirical literature on macro-economic environment and international trade.

Therefore, it is important to empirically analyse the factors and issues that affect and influence the services exports of the country. In this chapter an attempt has been made to study the major determinants of services exports of India during 2000-12. No doubt numerous factors and issues influence the services exports of the country but in the present study four major determinants viz. gross domestic product, human development index (HDI), exchange rate and tele-density have been discussed and probed in-depth. GDP represents the size of the economy as well as growth of the economy. HDI represents the average of per capita income of the country, health of the residents and educational attainments. Advances in the technology especially information technology and communications have been represented by the tele-density. Exchange rate represents the issues and relations of the external sector of the economy. The specification of these is as follows:

Gross Domestic Product: Size of the GDP and its growth over the period of time in an open economy generates much needed foreign exchange reserves by exporting production. Empirically, the studies on the subject have confirmed the positive impact of GDP on exports growth and expansion (Kumar, 1998; Majeed and Ahmad, 2006), so positive impact of GDP on services exports is expected. Further, the economic strength of an economy is gauged from the level of GDP and its growth and also that of per capita income over time. Moreover, higher levels of these two factors boost the service sector and are expected to play an important role in the performance of services exports of any economy. The level of GDP, GDP growth and per capita income are variables which move in same direction facilitated by one another. Therefore, including all these three variables exclusively as explanatory variables may pose severe multi co-linearity problem as the correlation among these variables is very high. Therefore, GDP as a variable is exclusively introduced as explanatory variable and other two are dropped purposely. So, in the present investigation first variable is GDP as determinant to explain the growth in exports of services.

Human Development: Optimum utilisation of human resources depends upon the level of human resource development (HRD) which positively impact GDP, its growth and in turn supports the expansion of exports (Majeed and Ahmad, 2006).

Many studies have justified the positive impact of HRD on exports (Pfaffermayr, 1996) and in the present case it is also expected that HRD positively contribute to the exports of services. Size, quality and growth of human capital may help an economy to produce quality services at competitive rates. India is having large proportion of population in productive age which appears to be the strength of the economy. Moreover, mushroom growth of technical education imparting institutions may improve the quality of this productive population. We expect that this human capital may contribute positively in the production of services in general and exports in particular. Therefore, human development index variable (HDI) has been identified to represent human development. Hence, it is included as explanatory variable to explain the export performance of services.

Exchange Rate: Under the World Trade Organisation regime, the principle of most favoured nation takes in its ambit the trade in services. Therefore, discretionary tariffs or other measures that impact the import and export of services to the member countries is close to impossible. Therefore, demand and supply are basically the only factors that can determine the export of service from a country. Therefore, the variables which have direct or indirect bearing on international capital movement may impact the movement of service. Therefore, trading partners want to keep their exchange rate in adequate price band. Very high foreign exchange rate depresses the competitiveness and a very low foreign exchange rate increases the import bill (Majeed and Ahmad, 2006). If these imports are used in the production of services then cost effectiveness of service sector will suffer. Foreign direct investment (FDI) and foreign exchange reserves are also positively correlated and affect the foreign exchange rate which is determined by demand and supply forces in international market. Hence, the capital movement in any format affects the foreign exchange rate. Therefore, to capture the impact of all these variables on the exports of services foreign exchange rate has been identified as a variable to explain export performance of services.

Tele-Density: Technological innovations such as number of televisions, computers, telephones, internet connections, etc., have important role to play in reducing the cost of production or/and improve the quality of the product. So, economies with better technical innovations may be able to improve its competitiveness and sustainability. Technological innovations and export performance bears positive significant relationship (Kumar, 1998; Majeed and Ahmad, 2006). Therefore, any proxy variable representing the technology should be included while modeling the services export performance. Though, R&D expenditure of Indian economy is very low and is not much contributing to the creation of innovations that seems to be the forte of developed countries. But, Indian mind is very sharp in adaptation of new technologies. Innovations of computer and user friendly technology have provided an edge to Indian users. More adaptability to the technology is directly reflected in the better performance of service sector and export of services. In the world of smart phones where lot of information is available in the hands of users, tele-density can act as an instrumental variable to represent the technology adaptation. Therefore, level of tele-density has been used as explanatory variable to explain the export service performance.

Due to the scope of the study and limited time framework other factors and issues have not been taken up for analysis. The detailed discussion and analysis of service category and code wise exports of services and their major determinants; tele-density, human development index (HDI), foreign exchange rate and gross domestic product (GDP) have been provided in the following sections of this chapter.

6.2.1 *The Modelling: Specification and Description*

Forgoing theoretical underpinning has helped us to develop the following model:

$$X_1 = f(X_2, X_3, X_4, X_5)$$

Where;

X_1 : Share of export services

X_2 : Tele-density

X_3 : Human Development Index (HDI)

X_4 : Foreign Exchange Rate (FER)

X_5 : Gross Domestic Product (GDP)

Hence, the following linear multiple regression model has been formulated:

$$X_{1t} = \beta_1 + \beta_2 X_{2t} + \beta_3 X_{3t} + \beta_4 X_{4t} + \beta_5 X_{5t} + e \qquad ...(6.1)$$

Here, β_1 is constant and β_2, β_3, β_4 and β_5 are coefficients of respective variables.

This model has been formulated from the general perception derived from the theoretical discussion made in preceding paragraphs. However, given the nature of service the weight-age of these variables may vary from service to service. Therefore, this equation has been estimated for total and individual services separately.

Generally, as already discussed GDP and HDI are expected to bear positive relationship with exports of services. Further, performance of technology variable may depend on the technology sensitiveness of the service. Exchange rate is expected to bear negative relationship with exports in services.

The estimation of this equation is based on the annual data from 2000 to 2012. Selection of time period and frequency of data are dictated by the availability of data from official sources. Since, the service classification by UNCTAD has been started in 2000 and before 2000 such classification was not available that is why the period of analysis has been reduced to 13 years. Keeping in view the length of the data an effort has been made in this model to concise the explanatory variables without compromising the strength of the model.

6.3 Results and Discussion

6.3.1 *Aggregate Services*

Performance of Indian aggregate services exports has been analysed in this section. In this context, equation 6.1 has been estimated for share in world services exports and share in total exports of India as dependent variables. The results are presented in Table 6.1.

Table 6.1: Determinants of Total Services Exports of India, 2000-2012

Panel - A	*Dependent Variable: share in world services exports (Case 1)*		
Variables	**Coefficient**	**t-Value**	**p-Value**
Constant	0.042	0.024	0.981
Tele-density	–0.697	–3.795	0.005
HDI	–0.049	–0.334	0.747
Exchange Rate	–0.114	–2.456	0.040
GDP	1.706	6.499	0.000
R^2 0.987 F-Value 150.390 (0.000)		D-W 1.814 N 13	
Panel - B	***Dependent Variable: share in total exports of India (Case 2)***		
Variables	**Coefficient**	**t-Value**	**p-Value**
Constant	25.074	1.324	0.222
Tele-density	–3.188	–6.469	0.000
HDI	–0.464	–1.184	0.274
Exchange Rate	0.005	0.044	0.966
GDP	4.044	5.746	0.000
R^2 0.906 F-Value 19.196 (0.000)		D-W 1.702 N 13	

When the variable share in world services exports has been used as dependent variable results are reported in panel A of the Table 6.1 and when share in total exports of India has been used as dependent variable results are presented in panel B of the Table 6.1. The entire table reveals that model specification is of very good quality as F statistic in both the cases is highly significant, that is, variables jointly explain the dependent variable. Therefore, the model is justified. Moreover, the values of D-W statistics indicate that no autocorrelation problem is present. And, the multi co-linearity problem has already been taken care while formulating the model. Besides, this has further been corroborated by the fact that explanatory power of the model is more than 90 per cent (R^2 = 0.987, Case 1 and R^2 = 0.906, Case 2). As expected variable GDP has turned out to be highly positive significant in both the cases meaning thereby, GDP growth is positively reflecting in India aggregate services exports performance. This indicates the fact that GDP growth and services exports are positively correlated. So far as the exchange rate and service exports are concerned, this variable as expected in theory is negatively significant in Case 1. However, this variable is insignificant in Case 2. Negative significant value of exchange rate in panel A is in accordance with theory but why this variable turned out insignificant in panel B. This may be due to the fact that the share of services in total exports is less and the effect may have been blurred due to examination of total aggregate services. Elasticity of exports of services needs further investigation. As there is lot of appreciation for Indian human development to contribute in service exports contrary to this fact this variable turned out insignificant. This may be either due to the quality of human development which is reported to be very weak or the potential of this resource is yet to be exploited. As already stated India is very poor in production of technology but very good in adaptation of technology; but adaptation of technology in improving services exports performance could not be verified. Rather, it laid its role negatively as in both the cases coefficient of tele-density is negatively significant (–0.697, Case 1 and –3.188, Case 2).

6.3.2 *Transportation Services*

This service category includes all transportation services that involve carriage of passengers, movement of goods (freight), rentals with crew, and related supporting services. Higher level of growth in any economy is accompanied by larger transportation equipments, vehicles and network, hence, higher potential of export of this service. The determinants of export of this service has been worked out by using equation 6.1 and by taking share of this service in total services exports of India and share in total exports of India as dependent variables. Model is justified by significant values of F statistics in both the cases and the model is free from autocorrelation as DW statistic value is close to 2 and explanatory power is also very high ($R^2 = 0.718$, Case 1 and $R^2 = 0.823$, Case 2). It can be hypothesized here that higher GDP is accompanied by higher transportation services. Therefore, GDP variable may be positively linked to export of this service. Table 6.2 reveals that GDP variable turned out positively significant in both the cases and in consonance with the theory. Since, transportation service do not require high quality of human capital therefore, this variable has no significant contribution in this service export as HDI variable turned out insignificant in both the cases. However, technological adaptation is very important in this service as this variable turned out significant in both the cases. Besides export of this service is linked to the physical production and do not bear any considerable connection with exchange rate as exchange rate variable is insignificant in both the cases.

Table 6.2: Determinants of Transportation Services Exports of India, 2000-2012

Panel - A	***Dependent Variable: share in total services exports (Case 1)***		
Variables	**Coefficient**	**t-Value**	**p-Value**
Constant	6.787	0.893	0.398
Tele-density	2.752	3.233	0.012
HDI	0.577	0.853	0.418
Exchange Rate	0.291	1.347	0.215
GDP	3.296	2.710	0.027
R^2 0.718		D-W 2.381	
F-Value 5.100	(0.024)	N 13	

Panel - B	*Dependent Variable: share in total exports (Case 2)*		
Variables	Coefficient	t-Value	p-Value
Constant	1.574	0.766	0.465
Tele-density	2.042	3.021	0.017
HDI	–0.203	–0.377	0.716
Exchange Rate	0.293	1.709	0.126
GDP	2.879	2.983	0.018
R^2 0.823 F-Value 9.270 (0.004)		D-W 2.341 N 13	

6.3.3 *Travel Service*

Since this service includes goods and services acquired by non-resident travellers during their visits this is a derivative form of service derived from the performance of other sectors. So, this service is expected to depend on very small factors which might not be captured under the explanatory variables included. This has been proved exclusively in the estimation of model. For instance, in both the cases constant value is highly significant. Even then we can continue with this model because no model specification arises as F statistics justifies the model and explanatory power is more than 80 per cent in both the cases. Moreover, serial correlation problem does not arise. This service export proved to be negatively associated with GDP as the GDP coefficient turned out negative in Case 1 and insignificant in Case 2. As already stated this service is derived from performance of other sectors so the level of HDI and exchange rate may become ineffective. Table 6.3 expound that both the variables are insignificant. However, tele-density variable is positively significant which reveals that adaptation of technology improves the travel services exports.

Table 6.3: Determinants of Travel Services Exports of India, 2000-2012

Panel - A	*Dependent Variable: share in total services exports (Case 1)*		
Variables	**Coefficient**	**t-Value**	**p-Value**
Constant	60.007	4.133	0.003
Tele-density	1.916	4.775	0.001
HDI	–0.491	–1.539	0.162
Exchange Rate	0.013	0.124	0.904
GDP	–2.171	–3.787	0.005
R^2 0.937 F-Value 29.947 (0.000)		D-W 2.250 N 13	
Panel - B	*Dependent Variable: share in total exports (Case 2)*		
Variables	**Coefficient**	**t-Value**	**p-Value**
Constant	16.415	3.415	0.009
Tele-density	0.671	0.970	0.045
HDI	–1.002	–1.823	0.106
Exchange Rate	0.008	0.046	0.964
GDP	–0.507	–0.513	0.622
R^2 0.814 F-Value 8.757 (0.005)		D-W 2.214 N 13	

6.3.4 *Communication Services*

This service includes postal, courier and telecommunications services between residents and non-residents. This service could not grew much in Indian setup rather with the growth of the economy India could not develop its competitiveness consequently, export in this service turned out negative significant which is a matter of serious concern and should be taken care by policy support. Performance of GDP variable automatically explains the insignificance of other three variables in the model, namely exchange rate, tele-density and HDI. And the results are true in both the cases. In spite of that model is justified and explanatory power is remarkable.

Table 6.4: Determinants of Communication Services Exports of India, 2000-2012

Panel - A	*Dependent Variable: share in total services exports (Case 1)*		
Variables	**Coefficient**	**t-Value**	**p-Value**
Constant	–14.992	–1.489	0.175
Tele-density	0.732	1.211	0.261
HDI	1.040	2.166	0.062
Exchange Rate	0.076	0.498	0.632
GDP	–2.575	–2.983	0.018
R^2 0.858 F-Value 12.089 (0.002)		D-W 1.882 N 13	
Panel - B	*Dependent Variable: share in total exports (Case 2)*		
Variables	**Coefficient**	**t-Value**	**p-Value**
Constant	–4.249	–1.441	0.188
Tele-density	–0.088	–0.133	0.897
HDI	0.983	1.866	0.099
Exchange Rate	0.072	0.429	0.680
GDP	–1.722	–1.819	0.106
R^2 0.829 F-Value 9.719 (0.004)		D-W 1.920 N 13	

6.3.5 *Construction Service*

Construction services exports covers the work performed on construction projects and installations by an enterprise outside the economy of residence of that enterprise. Export of construction service depend more on development of other countries therefore, much of the technological development and human resources may be depending on the receiving country as compared to India. Undoubtedly, generally growth of construction companies and acquiring expertise depend on their performance in domestic economy hence, the potential of construction services exports may depend positively on the overall growth acquired by the economy. In this context, Table 6.5 reports positive and significant coefficient of GDP variable in both the cases. Constant is significant in both the cases explained by the fact that this service depend more on the factors involving receiving country. Obviously, as a natural consequence technology adaptation and exchange rate turned out insignificant. However, HDI variable is beyond our comprehension or understanding and turned out negatively insignificant in both the cases. Besides, our model is justifiable (F value is significant), free from auto correlation and with high explanatory power.

Table 6.5: Determinants of Construction Services Exports of India, 2000-2012

Panel - A	*Dependent Variable: share in total services exports (Case 1)*		
Variables	Coefficient	t-Value	p-Value
Constant	29.421	6.453	0.000
Tele-density	–0.098	–0.168	0.871
HDI	–2.640	–5.695	0.000
Exchange Rate	0.005	0.032	0.975
GDP	2.109	2.531	0.035
R^2 0.868		D-W 2.346	
F-Value 13.124 (0.001)		N 13	

Panel - B	*Dependent Variable: share in total exports (Case 2)*		
Variables	Coefficient	t-Value	p-Value
Constant	8.155	6.042	0.000
Tele-density	–0.619	–0.976	0.358
HDI	–2.772	–5.498	0.001
Exchange Rate	0.012	0.078	0.940
GDP	2.778	3.067	0.015
R^2 0.844 F-Value 10.792 (0.003)		D-W 2.386 N 13	

6.3.6 *Insurance and Financial Services*

Insurance services cover all types of insurance, reinsurance and related auxiliary services. And, financial services include financial intermediation and auxiliary services, except those directly related to life insurance and pension funds (covered under insurance services). India's insurance and financial services are relatively less developed as compared to the developed countries. Developed countries are vigorously inclined to export the services to developing countries. Due to several factors like lack of capital infusion, want of innovative products these services are not of international standard in India hence, they are unable to withstand facilities available with other countries. Though, these services are included in the study for information purpose and to trigger the government for favourable policy environment but considerable result has been derived so far as determinants of insurance and financial services exports are concerned. Consequently unexplainable results to display only are presented in Tables 6.6 and 6.7 respectively.

Table 6.6: Determinants of Insurance Services Exports of India, 2000-2012

Panel - A	*Dependent Variable: share in total services exports (Case 1)*		
Variables	Coefficient	t-Value	p-Value
Constant	–0.122	–0.036	0.972

Tele-density	0.774	0.514	0.621
HDI	0.925	0.773	0.462
Exchange Rate	–0.175	–0.459	0.659
GDP	–1.797	–0.835	0.428
R^2 0.118 F-Value 0.268 (0.890)		D-W 2.088 N 13	
Panel - B	*Dependent Variable: share in total exports (Case 2)*		
Variables	**Coefficient**	**t-Value**	**p-Value**
Constant	–0.030	–0.023	0.982
Tele-density	–1.589	–1.175	0.274
HDI	0.278	0.259	0.802
Exchange Rate	–0.127	–0.370	0.721
GDP	1.482	0.767	0.465
R^2 0.289 F-Value 0.811 (0.552)		D-W 1.994 N 13	

Table 6.7: Determinants of Financial Services Exports of India, 2000-2012

Panel - A	*Dependent Variable: share in total services exports (Case 1)*		
Variables	**Coefficient**	**t-Value**	**p-Value**
Constant	–5.836	–0.432	0.677
Tele-density	–0.763	–0.843	0.424
HDI	0.194	0.269	0.794
Exchange Rate	–0.044	–0.191	0.853
GDP	1.351	1.046	0.326

R^2 0.682 F-Value 4.299 (0.038)		D-W 1.529 N 13	
Panel - B	***Dependent Variable: share in total exports (Case 2)***		
Variables	**Coefficient**	**t-Value**	**p-Value**
Constant	–1.778	–0.418	0.687
Tele-density	–1.378	–1.767	0.115
HDI	0.020	0.031	0.976
Exchange Rate	–0.024	–0.121	0.906
GDP	2.109	1.893	0.095
R^2 0.764 F-Value 6.462 (0.013)		D-W 1.424 N 13	

6.3.7 *Computer and Information Services*

Computer and information services of India have registered an increase in professionalism and Indian software industry is now recognised on global platform. The increased growth of computer and information services has directly impacted the national income and growth of GDP of the country (Kumar, 2001). Computer services consist of hardware and software-related services. And data processing and information services cover database services: database conception, data storage and dissemination of data. Direct non-bulk subscriptions to periodicals regardless of means of information transmission also belong to this service category. This is an important service which India exports to other countries. It commands more than 30 per cent of the service exports from India. Though, India could not maintain momentum that it achieved in the starting. Therefore, there are lot of under currents which need to be examined in this particular service. In this context equation 6.1 has been estimated for both the cases, that is, share in total services exports and share in total exports as dependent variable. The results are presented in Table 6.8.

Table 6.8: Determinants of Computer and Information Services Exports of India, 2000-2012

Panel - A	*Dependent Variable: share in total services exports (Case 1)*		
Variables	Coefficient	t-Value	p-Value
Constant	–104.705	–5.326	0.001
Tele-density	–0.021	–0.035	0.973
HDI	2.763	5.918	0.000
Exchange Rate	0.292	1.961	0.049
GDP	2.433	2.900	0.020
R^2 0.866 F-Value 12.916 (0.001)		D-W 1.745 N 13	
Panel - B	*Dependent Variable: share in total exports (Case 2)*		
Variables	Coefficient	t-Value	p-Value
Constant	–30.437	–6.293	0.000
Tele-density	–2.488	–0.318	0.654
HDI	1.228	5.165	0.001
Exchange Rate	0.193	2.541	0.035
GDP	1.754	4.107	0.003
R^2 0.965 F-Value 55.531 (0.000)		D-W 1.891 N 13	

Panel - A and Panel - B in Table 6.8 reveals significant F statistics value for the model meaning thereby, the model is justified. In other words explanatory variables jointly explain the variation in service exports over time. Besides the model is free from the problem of autocorrelation as the DW value is close to 2. Model specification has further been defended by the explanatory power in both the cases (R^2 = 0.866, Case 1 and R^2 = 0.965, Case 2). As India tread on high growth path and many other factors in its favour this service is positively linked to GDP growth. Undoubtedly, as Table 6.8 shows that GDP turned out positively significant variable in explaining the service exports in both the cases. Human development index reports positive significant coefficient meaning thereby, computer and information services are supported by human development in India. This is true in both the cases. Since, computer and information services accounts for very large share in total services exports the change in exchange rate have direct bearing on export of this service. Accordingly the variable turned significant. Moreover, technology adaptation did not play any considerable role.

One important feature of export of this service revealed by this table is in spite of having strong explanatory power and model justification the value of constant turned out to be negatively significant meaning thereby, apart from explanatory variables included there are some social, legal and psychological factors that discourage the export of this service. Apart from economic issues the state should take care of these issues.

6.3.8 *Royalties and License Fees*

Royalties and license fees covers franchising fees, royalties paid for the use of registered trademarks, and other fees paid for authorised use of intangible, non-produced and non-financial assets and proprietary rights. It is one of India's modern services and its share in total services exports of India is very low. India has not been able to improve and grow in this particular category of services exports and lags behind other developed countries. The intellectual properties rights in India are not strong and fail to protect the intellectual property. This may be one of the reasons for poor development of this sector. Though, this service is included in the study for information purpose but no considerable results have been derived so far as determinants of royalties and license fees services exports are concerned. Consequently unexplainable results to display only are presented in Table 6.9.

Table 6.9: Determinants of Royalties and License Fees Services Exports of India, 2000-2012

Panel - A	*Dependent Variable: share in total services exports (Case 1)*		
Variables	**Coefficient**	**t-Value**	**p-Value**
Constant	5.060	3.678	0.006
Tele-density	0.384	0.392	0.705
HDI	–2.422	–3.107	0.015
Exchange Rate	–0.093	–0.374	0.718
GDP	1.779	1.269	0.240
R^2 0.626 F-Value 3.350 (0.068)		D-W 2.973 N 13	
Panel - B	*Dependent Variable: share in total exports (Case 2)*		
Variables	**Coefficient**	**t-Value**	**p-Value**
Constant	1.405	3.145	0.014
Tele-density	0.003	0.003	0.998
HDI	–2.348	–2.694	0.027
Exchange Rate	–0.113	–0.407	0.695
GDP	2.152	1.373	0.207
R^2 0.532 F-Value 2.278 (0.150)		D-W 3.020 N 13	

6.3.9 *Other Business Services*

This service includes merchandising and other trade-related services; operational leasing services; and miscellaneous business, professional and technical services (legal, advertising, consultancy, accounting, R&D, etc.). Since, these services need expertise hence, may not be explained by model specified in equation 6.1. Though, it is expected that expertise may be better in high GDP and high HDI countries. But this does not hold true in case of India because these are more of academic activities and need brainy skills as compared to technology adaption or change in exchange rate. Basically this service involves the intellectual service. Therefore, this may be little bit free from technology adaptation, HDI and level of exchange rate. However, GDP level may be directly related to export of these professional services.

Table 6.10: Determinants of Other Business Services Exports of India, 2000-2012

Panel - A	*Dependent Variable: share in total services exports (Case 1)*		
Variables	**Coefficient**	**t-Value**	**p-Value**
Constant	36.722	1.077	0.313
Tele-density	–2.111	–1.788	0.112
HDI	–0.268	–0.286	0.782
Exchange Rate	–0.092	–0.308	0.766
GDP	1.954	2.159	0.049
R^2 0.458		D-W 1.352	
F-Value 1.691 (0.244)		N 13	
Panel - B	*Dependent Variable: share in total exports (Case 2)*		
Variables	**Coefficient**	**t-Value**	**p-Value**
Constant	11.370	0.856	0.417
Tele-density	–3.121	–3.271	0.011
HDI	–0.466	–0.614	0.556
Exchange Rate	0.032	0.134	0.897
GDP	3.207	2.353	0.046
R^2 0.646		D-W 1.362	
F-Value 3.653 (0.056)		N 13	

We are not surprised for getting such results in Table 6.10. The results show accordingly that the model is not justified and explanatory power is also not very good and model also suffers from autocorrelation and all the important variables are insignificant. Therefore, this service cannot be explained with the model specified in equation 6.1. Only personal characteristics of the personals need to be examined. Therefore, determinants of exports of these services cannot be explained with the secondary data domain and need fresh specification with data collected directly from the people in this category. Though, this service commands significant share in total services exports it is beyond the scope of present endeavour. Since, this service is an important source of foreign exchange the state should come forward to determine the factors and encourage this service for better and healthy export environment for this service.

6.3.10 *Personal, Cultural and Recreational Services*

Personal, cultural and recreational services include audiovisual and related services which cover the production of motion pictures; video and radio programmes, musical readings (and similar) including fees paid to personnel involved. Fees paid for sporting, theatrical and similar events belong to this category as well. Other personal, cultural and recreational services encompass services associated with museums, libraries, archives, and other cultural and sporting activities. Education and health services are covered under this category. Since every country make a cultural policy to protect the culture of the society therefore these services to grow take institutional support and cultural environment around. Therefore, higher GDP may contribute better to this service. Hence Table 6.11 reveals that coefficient of GDP turned out positively significant. This type of service export is free from exchange rate reason being such services are assignment based. Whenever a person or institution receives such an assignment then rate of exchange at that time becomes ineffective. Accordingly coefficient of exchange rate variable turned out insignificant in both the cases. Cultural and recreational services are produced from to some extent innate capability of personals and it does not matter whether HDI is low or high. Even some times uneducated or less educated persons may be able to contribute more in cultural and recreational services. Hence HDI bears insignificant coefficient. In modern days numbers of recreational instruments are technology based and adaptation to that technology may improve the performance of performers. Therefore, as expected technology adaptation bears positive significant coefficient in Table 6.11 in both the cases. Besides, model is justified and explanatory power is close to 80 per cent and autocorrelation has also not been diagnosed.

Table 6.11: Determinants of Personal, Cultural and Recreational Services Exports of India, 2000-2012

Panel - A	*Dependent Variable: share in total services exports (Case 1)*		
Variables	Coefficient	t-Value	p-Value
Constant	–0.202	–0.115	0.912
Tele-density	2.632	3.488	0.008
HDI	–0.419	–0.699	0.504
Exchange Rate	0.057	0.300	0.772
GDP	3.544	3.288	0.011
R^2 0.779 F-Value 7.036 (0.010)		D-W 1.685 N 13	
Panel - B	*Dependent Variable: share in total exports (Case 2)*		
Variables	Coefficient	t-Value	p-Value
Constant	–0.089	–0.143	0.890
Tele-density	2.822	3.759	0.006
HDI	–0.445	–0.746	0.477
Exchange Rate	0.078	0.411	0.692
GDP	3.705	3.455	0.009
R^2 0.781 F-Value 7.133 (0.009)		D-W 1.666 N 13	

6.3.11 *Government Services*

This service includes embassies, consulates, military units, transactions of international organisations, etc. These services are basically strategically more important rather than economically. The export of these services rather may depend on bilateral and multi-lateral relations among the nations and most of the times these services are exported to show the strategic and diplomatic strength. For instance Bangladesh and Pakistan are relatively weak in economic parameters but still they are performing better on these services exports. So far as concerned it is not exception. Table 6.12 reveals that constant is significant which justifies our fore-mentioned statement. Besides, economically better equipped country may have better capacity to export these strategic services. This is true for India as coefficient of GDP is positively significant in both the cases. Since, strategic and diplomatic services exports are not linked directly to HDI and exchange rate therefore, these factors did not play any role in government services exports in India as coefficient of HDI and exchange are insignificant. Adaptation to technology may improve the performance of these services. Consequently, better performance has been reported in exports of government services. Therefore, in Indian setup this variable has turned out with positive significant coefficient. Moreover, this model is justified by highly significant F-value and more than 80 per cent explanatory power. Moreover, auto correlation does not create any problem here.

Table 6.12: Determinants of Government Services Exports of India, 2000-2012

Panel - A	*Dependent Variable: share in total services exports (Case 1)*		
Variables	Coefficient	t-Value	p-Value
Constant	24.294	2.646	0.029
Tele-density	1.810	2.669	0.028
HDI	–0.833	–1.545	0.161
Exchange Rate	–0.033	–0.191	0.853

GDP	1.636	1.689	0.049
R^2 0.821 F-Value 9.189 (0.004)		Durban-Watson Statistic 1.901 N 13	
Panel - B	***Dependent Variable: share in total exports (Case 2)***		
Variables	**Coefficient**	**t-Value**	**p-Value**
Constant	6.697	2.681	0.028
Tele-density	1.727	2.524	0.036
HDI	–0.863	–1.588	0.151
Exchange Rate	–0.037	–0.212	0.838
GDP	1.536	1.571	0.050
R^2 0.818 F-Value 8.995 (0.005)		D-W 1.989 N 13	

To sum up, the above analysis clearly brought out that many factors and issues affect and influence the services exports of the country. Though, numerous factors and issues influence the services exports of the country but gross domestic product, human development index (HDI), exchange rate and tele-density have been discussed and probed in-depth. Regression results of these determinants as dependent variables of various services exports have been presented in Table 6.13.

Table 6.13: Regression Results of Determinants of Various Services Exports of India

Services	Case	Constant	Tele-density	HDI	Exchange Rate	GDP
Aggregate services	*Case 1* *Case 2*		× ×	– –	× –	✓ ✓
Transportation services	*Case 1* *Case 2*		✓ ✓	– –	– –	✓ ✓
Travel services	*Case 1* *Case 2*	✓ ✓	✓ ✓	– –	– –	× –

Communication services	*Case 1* *Case 2*		– –	– –	– –	– –
Construction services	*Case 1* *Case 2*	✓ ✓	– –	× ×	– –	✓ ✓
Insurance services	*Case 1* *Case 2*		– –	– –	– –	– –
Financial services	*Case 1* *Case 2*		– –	– –	– –	– –
Computer and Information services	*Case 1* *Case 2*	× ×	– –	✓ ✓	✓ ✓	✓ ✓
Royalties and license fees	*Case 1* *Case 2*		–	– –	– –	– –
Other business services	*Case 1* *Case 2*		– –	– –	– –	✓ ✓
Personal, cultural and recreational services	*Case 1* *Case 2*		✓ ✓	– –	– –	✓ ✓
Government services	*Case 1* *Case 2*	✓ ✓	✓ ✓	– –	– –	✓ ✓

Note: 1. × stands for negatively significant, 2. ✓ stands for positively significant, 3. – stands for insignificant.

In case of total services exports of India the GDP coefficient was positively significant. This means that the economic strength of the country positively contributes to exports of services. In case of exchange rate, in the first case it is negatively significant and in the second case it is insignificant. For HDI in both the cases it is insignificant. And lastly in case of tele-density in both the cases it is negatively significant.

In case of transportation services exports both the tele-density coefficient and GDP coefficient are positively significant in both the cases. This means that economic growth and technological advancement in the country contributes positively to the exports of transportation services. For HDI coefficient and exchange rate coefficient both turned out to be insignificant in both the cases and hence it depicts that human development and exchange rate have no impact on exports of transportation services in case of India.

In travel services exports the tele-density coefficient is positively significant and hence advancement of technology in case of India positively contributes to exports of travel services. All the other coefficients are insignificant for travel services; hence exports of travel services do not require good quality human resources and exchange rates do not affect exports of this service. It is noted that in case of exports of travel services the constant appeared to be positively significant in both the cases which means that there may be other factors besides the ones being discussed that explain the performance of this service.

In case of India's communication services exports all the coefficients appeared to be insignificant in both the cases.

For construction services, the economic growth of India has positively contributed to the development of this service. India's economic growth and development has helped it to acquire more construction projects in foreign lands and hence, the positive relationship. Exchange rate and tele-density do not affect the growth of this service as they are insignificant. But, in case of HDI, more qualified the human capital, less employable in construction work. Hence, the HDI coefficient turned out to be negatively significant in case of India's construction services exports. Also the constant turned out to be positively significant in this case which means that this service is dependent more on factors involving the receiving country and hence, the constant is positive.

In case of insurance and financial services exports of India, the results for these two services show that India lags behind in exports of these two services. Due to factors like lack of innovative products, lack of capital infusion, etc., insurance and financial services exports of India are not of international standards and hence India's performance in these services is not good.

For computer and information services the HDI coefficient, exchange rate coefficient and GDP coefficient turned out to be positively significant. This means that higher the level of economic growth and human capital it positively affects the exports of computer and information services as this service requires good infrastructure and professionals with high skills. Since this service directly caters to the needs of foreign countries, the exchange rate also affects the growth of this service. Technological adaptation turned out to be insignificant in this case. But the constant for this service was negatively significant, which means that apart from the factors being discussed here there are some other social, legal and psychological factors that negatively affect the export of this service.

In case of other business services only GDP coefficient turned out to be positively significant and hence higher the economic growth of India higher would be the performance of this service. The rest of the three variables are insignificant as this type of service depends more on the personal expertise of the person involved rather than other factors. This service includes professional business services like legal, advertising, consultancy, accounting, etc. so the person involved in this and his expertise in the field play an important role. Here, overall HDI of the country does not have any significance.

In case of personal, cultural and recreational services, India's overall economic growth and technological adaptation support the growth of this service and hence are significant. HDI and exchange rate hold insignificant relationship as those people who are interested in exploring the art and culture of India will visit and avail this service anyway irrespective of these two factors.

Government services are more strategically important to a country rather than economically. So, in this case HDI and exchange rate hold no significance. The overall economic development leads to more infrastructure and support to government services, and hence, it is significant in this case. Also, technological adaptation provides support and good infrastructure and hence bears positive significance. For government services the constant turned out to be positively significant because of the nature of the service. As already stated this service is more strategically important hence, there may be other factors which explain this service apart from the ones being discussed here.

Here, again the second hypothesis of the study holds true that India's services exports were supported by four major determinants namely size of the economy, technology, human resource development and international capital movement.

❐

Chapter 7

Summary, Findings and Policy Implications

7.1 Summary

Due to changing economic policies, the structure of Indian economy has experienced major shifts in sectoral distribution of Gross Domestic Product (GDP). The primary sector stagnated and its share in GDP has declined sharply and secondary sector gained less as compared to tertiary sector. Presently, the tertiary sector has been the major driver of the growth of Indian economy. The share of exports of services in the total exports of India has been increasing over the years. Therefore, Indian services exports are not only of vital importance in India's overall international trade but are also an important component of overall national economic growth. Among all the countries, in 2010, India ranked 10th from above in the exports of services and 20th in merchandised exports. Reforms in the trade policy of India have identified trade in services as a key and strategic sector under the export-led growth strategy. Government of India attempts to exploit the opportunities of trade in services and has setup a Service Export Promotion Council for the purpose. Further, policy also provides exemptions on taxes upon many exportable services. In India, the growth of service sector is almost along the global service market trends during neo-liberal regime, but there are two distinctive features of this growth firstly, the entire decline in the share of primary sector in GDP has been absorbed by the service sector and share of manufacturing remained the same. Secondly, in spite of the rising share of services in GDP and trade, there has not been a corresponding rise in the share of services in total employment, which has raised doubts about its sustainability. Therefore, it is of paramount importance to investigate the various dimensions of growth of services exports of the country.

The aim of the present study is to examine the growth and trends of services exports of India along with the composition, global competitiveness and performance of India in the services exports during the period 1995-2012. Present endeavour also attempts to examine the major determinants of India's exports of services, to identify the major managerial and policy issues impacting India's services exports and finally to suggest policy measures for further strengthening of exports of services. The study has been organized into seven chapters. The study has been organized into seven chapters. Chapter 1 includes the theory and concepts of services trade. Chapter 2 consists of theoretical issues of services sector of India, managerial issues and policy initiatives and approaches taken by government of India. Chapter 3 includes the perspectives of services exports of India. The growth and trends of India's international trade in services have been discussed in Chapter 4. Chapter 5 evaluates the competitiveness and performance of services exports of India. The major determinants of services exports of India have been presented in Chapter 6. And in the final chapter summary, findings and policy implications are listed.

India is one of the emerging countries whose economic growth in the recent years is the result of growth of services exports. The growing share of services in the GDP of India since 1995 clearly supports this evidence. During the Nehruvian-Mahalanobis led-growth strategy era, that is, 1950-51 to 1964-65 the share of primary sector declined in the total GDP of India and the share of secondary and tertiary sector increased in total GDP. During the industrial deceleration and agriculture led-growth strategy era from 1965-66 to 1979-80, the tertiary sector grew at an annual average growth rate of 4.4 per cent which was higher than the other two sectors. During the period 1980-81 to 1991-92 called the liberalisation and minimum needs led-growth strategy era tertiary sector grew at the highest annual average growth rate of 6.7 per cent followed by secondary and primary sectors. During the period 1992-93 to 2001-02 called the economic reforms led-growth strategy era again, the tertiary sector's growth was the highest with 8.4 per cent annual average growth rate followed by secondary and primary sectors. From 2001-02 to 2011-12 called the post economic reforms era the 9.5 per cent annual average growth rate of the tertiary sector was the highest.

Services are different from goods in many respects and thus they require different set of framework for analysis. The General Agreement of Trade in Services (GATS) provides the definition of services along with the theoretical framework for trade in services. According to this the tradability of services is divided into four modes of supply. These four modes include first, cross-border trade in which services are supplied from one country to another country with the buyers and sellers staying in their respective countries. Second is the consumption abroad mode in which buyer moves to the country of the seller to avail services. Third mode is the commercial presence mode in which the seller sets up office in the other country. Fourth, presence of natural persons mode in which an individual moves to the foreign country in order to provide services. Services are divided into 12 categories by United Nations Conference on Trade and Development (UNCTAD) and this is the standardized categorisation followed at international level.

The review of literature on the subject has been divided into six sub-parts; each part includes studies that are specific to a particular objective of the study. The studies in every part are organized in reverse chronological order, starting from the recent studies and moving towards the older studies. In the first part of the review of literature those studies are included which discuss the various concepts, definitions and GATS provisions and agreements of trade in services. The second part of the literature review includes studies which discuss and focus on composition of services, direction of trade in services and production and competitiveness of trade in services. The next part of the review consists of studies which study the impact of trade in services on economic growth of the country and poverty and employment related issues of trade in services. The next part of the literature includes studies which relate to issues related to specific services categories. The specific categories of services include services like computer and information services, transport services, educational services, insurance services, telecommunication services and health related services. The last part of the literature review includes the conclusions and research gaps that emerged after the study of literature.

The review of literature on international trade in services, regulations and provisions under GATS, composition, direction, competitiveness and exports of different types of services confirms that most of the research analysed and covered the role of individual services and their impact on Indian economy and world economy. Majority of them concentrated on GATS provisions, agreements, future negotiations, role in economic growth, GDP, and employment generation and particularly the role of IT, software and Business Process Outsourcing (BPO) services. Few studies explore the reciprocal inter-relations among services exports, economic growth, and comparative advantage of nation and employment issues exhaustively and comprehensively. Modernisation of economies lead to growth in income, this resulted in increased demand of services and hence growth of services sector. Further, due to introduction of new technologies in manufacturing sector, on one hand the need of intermediate or producer services increased and on the other hand there was a shift in the employment trend towards the services sector which further accelerated the growth of service sector. Some studies examined the factors that lead to increase of employment in services sector and investigate the relation between decreased productivity and employment in manufacturing sector and relative increase in productivity and employment of the services sector.

There are few studies that explore the distinguishing characteristics of goods and services and cover the modes of transaction in services exports. Factors like geography, accumulated knowledge of the local population, work experience, external environment like location of firms in large cities and pressure on private and semi-private sector to sell their services to new markets contributes to development of export advantages in some regions. Further, it is evidently clear that there seems a paucity of studies on exports of services at aggregate level, i.e. analysing the trends and impact of exports of services on economic growth and employment scenario of Indian economy.

International trade injects global competition and hence domestic industry tends to become competitive and efficient, therefore, international trade is very important and crucial for all the countries in the world. Recently, the issues of international trade and economic growth have gained substantial importance with the introduction of trade liberalisation policies. As a result of this, the volume of international trade has increased from US $ 6,338,858 billion in 1995 to US $ 22,662,355 billion in 2012. Empirical analysis of international trade has clearly established that international trade leads to economic growth provided the policy initiatives and infrastructure are accommodative to cope with the social, economic and financial changes at international level.

International trade plays a very important role as it increases global competition and hence the domestic sector also tries to improve and become competitive and efficient. The international trade of world in both goods and services has increased at an annual average growth rate of 8.8 per cent during the period 1995-2012. The growth of transition countries of the world has been the highest over the same period at 14.3 per cent. Developing countries followed with 11.7 per cent and developed countries recorded the lowest growth rate of 7 per cent for the period 1995-2012. The share of India's total exports in total world exports increased from 0.6 per cent in 1995 to 2 per cent in 2012 and registered an annual average growth rate of 17.7 per cent for the same period. India's services exports increased at an annual average growth rate of 22 per cent and registered better performance as compared to goods exports which recorded growth rate of 16.1 per cent for the same period. The analysis of services exports of BRICS showed that India was the largest country in services exports only after China in the year 2012.

The growing importance of Indian services can be supported by the fact that India grew at the highest annual average growth rate of 22 per cent among all the BRICS countries as well as the annual average growth rate of all the BRICS nations combined. The analysis of SAARC countries also shows the growing importance of India's exports of services. India contributed around 88 per cent of the total services exports of SAARC and was the largest exporter of services among the group in the year 2012. Here again India recorded the highest annual average growth rate of 22 per cent among all the countries and all the SAARC nations combined together for the period 1995-2012. The composition of services exports has been studied according to two different classifications of services along with codes provided by the UNCTAD. The classification from 1995-99 includes three services categories namely, travel services (02), transport services (01) and other commercial services (13). The second classification from 2000-12 includes 12 categories of services, namely (01) transport services; (02) travel services; (05) other services; (07) communication services; (06) construction services; (16) insurance services; (13) financial services; (10) computer and information services; (14) royalties and license fees services; (15) other business services; (18) personal, cultural and recreational services; and (21) government services. The study of composition of world services exports shows that the transport services, travel services and other business services comprise around 70 per cent of the total services exports for the year 2012. But the fastest growing services category is the computer and information services with 16.6 per cent annual average growth rate for the period 2000-12. In case of SAARC countries, the transport services, travel services; computer and information services and other business services comprise around 86 per cent of the total services exports of SAARC for the year 2012. The analysis of composition of BRICS countries also yielded similar results as around 88 per cent of the exports of services of BRICS were constituted by transport services, travel services, computer and information services and other business services for the year 2012. The study of composition of India's services exports shows that the other business services and computer and information services were the highest contributors with 32.9 per cent and 32.3 per cent shares in total services exports respectively for the year 2012. The analysis pointed out that there has been a shift in the services categories being exported and India is now exporting more non-traditional and modern services. The study of direction of total exports of India shows that a decline has been registered in exports to OECD countries and Eastern European countries and the exports to OPEC and developing countries has increased from 1995 to 2012.

The competitiveness and performance of services exports of India is calculated and evaluated and five indices and indicators have been used namely Observed Export Share (OES) index; Adjusted Export Share (AES) index; Openness Factor (OF) index; Revealed Comparative Advantage (RCA) index; and Comparative Export Performance (CEP) index. The analysis of country profile shows that India is the fourth largest country in size and second largest in population among all the BRICS and SAARC countries. India's poverty headcount is quite high and life expectancy was 66 years for the year 2012. In case of Human Development Index (HDI) India's rank was 135 and it came under medium human development index group of countries in the world for the year 2013.

The economic profile of all the countries shows that India was at fourth position with US $ 1.877 trillion GDP for the year 2012. For the year 2013, India's annual GDP growth percentage was 4.7 and India was at the fourth position. For the year 2012 India received 1.7 per cent of GDP as FDI net inflows.

The services trade profile of all the BRICS and SAARC countries reveals that India performed better than all the countries in exports of services for the year 2012 and registered a share of 3.3 per cent in total world exports of services only after China whose share was 4.3 per cent of the total world services exports for the same year. India was also the second largest importer of services for the year 2012 and registered a share of three per cent in total world imports of services. Here again China had the largest share at 6.6 per cent. The comparison of all the countries shows that India is one of the important and fast growing members of these two groups in terms of economic growth and services trade. India's trade performance in services is very impressive and it only lags behind China.

In order to evaluate the global competitiveness of countries 12 pillars approach is used in which scores are allocated against each pillar and also ranks are assigned according to these scores. Then the overall competitiveness is calculated by combining all the ranks and scores. India's overall position shows that India ranked 60 out of 148 countries in the world competitiveness index for the year 2013-14. India was above the middle mark but has a long way to go.

The comparison of annual average Observed Export Share index for the period 2000-12 reveals that among the BRICS and SAARC countries China had the highest share of 3.44 per cent in the total world services exports followed only by India with 2.43 per cent. The detailed analysis of category-wise services exports of India reveals that computer and information services recorded the highest share of 18.05 per cent in world exports of computer and information services for the year 2012. The other category of services that performed well was the other business services with 4.10 per cent share in total world exports of other business services.

The comparative annual average adjusted export share index of services exports for the period 2000-12 of India, BRICS and major SAARC countries show that for total services exports Sri Lanka performed better than all the other countries with the value of 206.18. India's performance was best in computer and information services as it recorded the value of 681.35 for the same period which was much higher than the value of all the other countries. Also, India's performance in other business services was good and India stood at third place with a value of 129.78. The detailed analysis of category-wise services exports of India showed that in India's export basket computer and information services and other business services have been performing better than all the other categories of services.

India's dependency on certain category of services trade is calculated by Openness Factor index. The openness factor index takes into account both the exports and imports of the category and then calculates the dependency on that particular category of product. The results show that India's dependency on overall services trade has almost doubled from 2000 to 2012. India's dependency on trade of services like transport services, financial services, travel services, computer and information services and other business services has also increased over the period of study. For the rest of the services categories the dependency either decreased or remained constant for the period 2000-12.

The analysis of Revealed Comparative Advantage index (RCA) of India with BRICS and major SAARC countries for different categories of services shows that India has advantage over all the other countries in exports of computer and information services. In case of other business services also India has export advantage over Russia, South Africa, Pakistan, Bangladesh and Sri Lanka out of all the seven countries (Brazil, Russia, China, South Africa, Pakistan, Bangladesh and Sri Lanka). In case of insurance services exports, India has comparative advantage over Brazil, Russia, China, Pakistan and Bangladesh. India's exports of personal, cultural and recreational services had comparative advantage over Brazil, China, Pakistan and Bangladesh.

Comparative export performance index is also used to measure the competitiveness in exports of services and it reveals export specialisation of a country in particular product. The comparison of India with other countries shows that India has specialisation in exports of computer and information services and other business services for the period 2000-12. The values of the index in case of financial services and personal, cultural and recreational services are small but highest for India. So, in these two services categories also India had specialisation as compared to other countries. The results of annual comparative export performance of India's services exports shows that India had specialisation in exports of computer and information services for the period 2000-12. It was followed by other business services, communication services and insurance services for the same period of study.

The literature indentified some determinants of services exports such as size of the economy, advances in technology, development of human capital, labour, exchange rate and overall economic growth. In order to empirically analyse the factors, four determinants have been selected, namely Gross Domestic Product (GDP), Human Development Index (HDI), exchange rate and tele-density. Using these four determinants multiple regressions are run and results are obtained for all the different categories of services. For the aggregate services exports of India, GDP was positively significant and HDI was insignificant. In case of transportation services, tele-density and GDP were positively significant. For travel services exports of India, tele-density was positively significant were as other three factors were insignificant. For communication services, all the factors turned out to be insignificant. For construction services, GDP was positively significant and HDI was negatively significant. The other two factors namely tele-density and exchange rate were insignificant. All the factors were insignificant for insurance services exports. Similarly, for financial services exports also all the factors were insignificant according to the results. For computer and information services exports, the HDI, exchange rate and GDP were positively significant and tele-density was insignificant. In case of royalties and license fees services, all the four factors were insignificant. For other business services, GDP was positively significant and the other three factors were insignificant. Tele-density and GDP both were significant for personal, cultural and recreational services whereas HDI and exchange rate were insignificant. And lastly for government services, tele-density and GDP were positively significant and HDI and exchange rate were insignificant.

Managerial and policy issues related to services exports suggest that the services sector in India is controlled and governed by multiple ministries and agencies. The services categories are divided under three lists and their jurisdiction is defined according to these three lists. The first list is called the union list and contains services categories that are controlled by Central Government of India. This includes services like telecommunications, postal, broadcasting, financial services such as insurance and banking and mining services. The second list called the state list consists of health care and related services, real estate services, retail services and agriculture, and hunting and forestry. These services are controlled and governed by state governments. The third list is called the concurrent list and the services coming in this list are governed and regulated by both central and state governments. The services include professional services, educational services, printing and publishing and electricity services.

Services in India are also classified on the basis of National Industrial Classification, 2008. This classification includes Section G: Wholesale and retail trade, repair of motor vehicles; Section H: Transportation and storage; Section I: Accommodation and Food service activities; Section J: Information and Communication; Section K: Financial and Insurance activities; Section L: Real Estate activities; Section M: Professional, Scientific and Technical activities; Section N: Administrative and Support Service activities; Section O: Public administration and defense, compulsory social security; Section P: Education; Section Q: Human health and social work activities; Section R: Arts, Entertainment and Recreation; Section S: Other Service activities; Section T: Activities of households as employers, undifferentiated goods and services producing activities of households for own use; and Section U: Activities of extra-territorial organisations and bodies.

At international level UNCTAD provides with the classification of services along with codes. Up to 1999 the classification of services included three categories, namely transport services (02), travel services (03), and other services (13). From the year 2000 UNCTAD changed the classification of services and included other categories of services and now there are 12 categories of services. These 12 categories include 01 - Transport; 02 - Travel; 05 - Other services; 07 - Communication; 06 - Construction; 16 - Insurance; 13 - Financial services; 10 - Computer and Information; 14 - Royalties and License Fees; 15 - Other Business services; 18 - Personal, Cultural and Recreational services; and 21 - Government services.

The analysis suggests that the managers of the services providing firms consider services marketing mix or extended marketing mix as one of the important determinants of services exports. This mix includes seven components, namely price, product, promotion, place, physical evidence, process and people. The literature on managerial perceptions regarding determinants of exports performance has also given some other important determinants. These determinants include service quality, competition degree, design of the product, brand image, distribution network and innovation.

The foreign trade policy of India is the backbone of Indian foreign trade and latest foreign trade policy of India, 2009-14 includes some very important schemes and innovative policy initiatives to support foreign trade, especially services exports. Some of the policy initiatives stressed upon market diversification, upgradation of technology, support to electronic and IT manufacturing industries, etc. The foreign trade policy also includes some specific schemes like Assistance to States for Developing Export Infrastructure and Allied Activities (ASIDE), Market Access Initiative (MAI), Market Development Assistance (MDA), and Town of Export Excellence (TEE) in order to support and encourage exports of India. There are also some policy initiatives that take care of quality of the products India is exporting and helps to maintain international standards. The policy must address the specific issues for services negotiations, general service policies of India to promote exports, market access and trade barriers for services policy-making, institutional set up and data issues related to trade in services.

Discussion of the important trade agreements that India has signed with countries of the world to promote foreign trade from 1995 points out that in all there are 20 such important trade agreements focusing on liberalising trade among countries. India has signed a number of trade agreements with African countries over the time. These trade agreements include lowering of trade barriers and facilitating trade with various African countries. These trade agreements have helped African countries to increase their foreign trade and hence improve economic health and helped India to further increase its exports and market access. India is also co-operating with a number of Asian countries and has signed nine trade agreements involving only Asian countries. The most important being the SAARC Agreement on Trade in Services (SATIS) signed in 2010. India is also focusing on its trade relations with Latin American countries and in order to boost trade ties with these countries India has signed trade agreements with individual countries as well as a trade agreement between India and MERCOSUR group of countries including Argentina, Brazil, Paraguay and Uruguay. India's trade agreements also include European partners like Finland.

7.2 Findings

- The primary sector of India stagnated and its share in GDP has declined sharply and secondary sector gained less as compared to tertiary sector. Presently, the tertiary sector has been the major driver of the growth of Indian economy. Further, the share of export of services in the total exports of India has been increasing over the years.
- The demand for services have increased due to modernisation of economies and hence growth of services sector.
- The demand for intermediate or producer services has increased over the period of study due to technological advances in manufacturing sector.
- The employment sector has experienced a shift towards services sector.
- Export advantages in some regions is experienced due to factors like geography, accumulated knowledge of the local population, work experience, location of the firms in large cities and pressure on private and semi-private sector to sell their services to new markets.
- International trade in goods and services has increased in volume and value.
- Transition countries of the world are growing faster than developed and developing countries in international trade in services.
- The provision of trade liberalisation and agreements of WTO and GATS have helped the growth of trade in goods as well as in services across the globe.

- On the basis of important indicators like share of India's services exports in total exports of India, share of services exports of India in world services exports and annual percentage change of services exports of India it can be concluded that exports of services are the future growth engine of Indian economy.
- Over the period of study 1995-2012, only India was able to increase its share of services among BRICS countries and share of other countries declined.
- India has emerged as the largest exporter of services among SAARC group of countries for the period 1999-2012.
- Advances in technologies of telecommunications, data processing and information dissemination have lead to increased tradability of non-traditional and modern services and hence a shift in composition of India's exports of services.
- The direction of total exports of India has changed towards OPEC and developing countries over the period of study.
- India has shown competitiveness and specialisation in exports of computer and information services and other business services in comparison to other BRICS and SAARC countries.
- India has registered competitiveness in total services exports in comparison to other BRICS and SAARC countries for the period 2000-12.
- India has shown potential for competitiveness in transportation services exports and communication services exports.
- India has registered revealed comparative advantage in exports of computer and information services exports as compared to other BRICS and SAARC countries for the period 2000-12.
- India's top performing services exports categories have been computer and information services exports followed

by other business services exports, communication services exports and insurance services exports.

- Empirical analysis of the services exports of India clearly establish that the first hypothesis of the study, India's services exports performed well than that of other suppliers in world market.
- Though numerous factors and issues influence the services exports of India but, GDP, HDI, exchange rate and tele-density have been the major ones which proves the acceptance of second hypothesis of the study.
- There is no universal classification of services available and different sources provide different classifications.
- Services marketing mix or the extended marketing mix have emerged as an important determinant of services export performance.

7.3 Policy Suggestions

Indian service exports are not only of importance in India's overall international trade but are also as an important component and instrument of overall national economic growth. In this light, the present study offers some policy initiatives for services policy-makers for strengthening the India's services exports in the future. The specific suggestions are as follows:

- The study points out that there is a dearth of research studies on the subject and it is suggested that more specific studies on India's services exports should be conducted.
- The analysis shows that in contrast to trade in goods and that of total world trade, the international trade in services has experienced less diversion. Therefore, it should be considered as a challenge before India and the country should explore possibilities of more exports of services to developing and transition economies across the globe.
- The study also points out that services exports seems to be the future growth engine of Indian economy and it

is recommended that India should increase its share of services exports in total exports.

- It emerged from the analysis that India is emerging as a hub of services exports among SAARC and BRICS countries. Therefore, it is suggested that India must invest in the service sector to build world class infrastructure and facilities to attract the services demand from every corner of the world.
- The experiences of exports of services of India show that the shares and growth of newly emerged services has increased. And it is suggested that right kind of policy intervention should be initiated to explore more services for export purposes.
- The analysis of various contributory pillars/factors of competitiveness of services exports of India suggest that India needs to do much more progress and to initiate policy measures on this front to compete globally.
- The numerous indicators and indices of competitiveness, openness, comparative advantage and specialisation suggest that India has better performance in many services. Therefore, it is recommended that India should also concentrate on the services that have been left behind such as royalties and license fees services; personal, cultural and recreational services and government services.
- Specifically, revealed comparative advantage index in case of computer and information services has been declining over the period of study. The study suggests that the cause for this trend should be explored and policy initiatives should be taken to maintain the stability of services exports.
- Study highlights that GDP, HDI, exchange rate and tele-density are the major determinants of services exports of India. In this light India must focus to increase its economic health and as well as concentrate upon various human development aspects. Also policies should be laid in place to maintain suitable exchange rate and

to increase the penetration of technologies as well as adaptation of new technologies.

- Apart from the above there are certain policy issues that India faces and requires urgent attention. These include data availability and ambiguity problem, lack of institutional setup to support exports of services, creation of new markets and increasing market access as well as reduction in trade barriers for services, policy issues related to negotiations in services trade and India's general service policies to promote exports.

❒

Bibliography

Adlung, Rudolf and Aaditya Matto (2008): "The GATS", Aaditya Mattoo, Robert M. Stern and Gianni Zanini (Eds.), *A Handbook of International Trade in Services*, Oxford University Press, New York, USA, pp. 48-83.

Anderson, Kym (2001): "Globalisation, WTO, and ASEAN", *ASEAN Economic Bulletin*, Vol. 18, No. 1, pp. 12-23.

Ansari, M.I. (1995): "Explaining the Services Sector Growth: An Empirical Study of India, Pakistan and Sri Lanka", *Journal of Asian Economics*, Vol. 6, No. 2, pp. 233-46.

Balassa, B. (1965): "Trade Liberalisation and Revealed Comparative Advantage", *The Manchester School of Economic and Social Studies,* Vol. 33, No. 2, pp. 99-123.

Balassa, B. (1977): "Revealed Comparative Advantage Revisited: An Analysis of Relative Export Shares of the Industrial Countries, 1953-1971", *Manchester School of Economic & Social Studies*, Vol. 45, No 4, pp. 327-44.

Banga, Rashmi (2005): "Critical Issues in India's Service-Led Growth", Working Paper No. 171, Indian Council for Research on International Economic Relations, New Delhi.

Banga, Rashmi (2005): "Role of Services in the Growth Process: A Survey", Working Paper, No. 159, Indian Council for Trade and International Economic Relations, New Delhi.

Banga, Rashmi and Bishwanath Goldar (2007): "Contribution of Services to Output Growth and Productivity in Indian

Manufacturing: Pre- and Post-Reforms", *Economic and Political Weekly*, Vol. 42, No. 26, pp. 2769-77.

Banga, Rashmi and Dinesh Kumar (2010): "India's Exports of Software Services: Role of External Demand and Productivity", *'Frontier Issues in Technology, Development and Environment'*, Annual Conference of IASSI, Madras School of Economics, March 2010, (www.mse.ac.in/Frontier/n14%20Rashmi.pdf).

Bhagwati, Jagdish, N. (1982): "Introduction to Import Competition and Response", *Import Competition and Response*, University of Chicago Press, Chicago, USA, pp. 1-8.

Bhagwati, Jagdish, N. (1984): "Splintering and Disembodiment of Services and Developing Nations", *World Economy*, Vol. 7, No. 2, pp. 133-43.

Bhagwati, Jagdish, N. (1985): "Why are Services Cheaper in the poor Countries?", in Gene Grossman (Ed.), *Wealth and Poverty*, Essays in Development Economics Series, Vol. 1. Cambridge, MIT Press, England, Blackwell, pp. 82-91.

Bhattacharya, B.B. and Arup Mitra (1990): "Excess Growth of Tertiary Sector in Indian Economy: Issues and Implications", *Economic and Political Weekly*, Vol. 25, No. 44, pp. 2445-50.

Chanda, Rupa (2002): *Globalisation of Services: India's Opportunities and Constraints*, Oxford University Press, New Delhi.

Chanda, Rupa (2003): "General Agreement on Trade in Services: Implications for Social Policy-making", *Economic and Political Weekly*, Vol. 38, No. 16, pp. 1567-78.

Chanda, Rupa (2005): "Trade in Services and South Asia: An Aggressive Agenda", in *South Asia Yearbook on Trade and Development 2005: Mainstreaming Development in Trade Negotiations; Run Up to Hong Kong,* (Ed.), 105-208, Centre for Trade and Development, New Delhi.

Chemsripong, Sujinda and Amir Mahmood (2008): "Services Exports: An Evolution and Evaluation of Thailand's Services Exports In The Context Of ASEAN-5", *International Business & Economics Research Journal,* Vol. 7, No. 9, pp. 27-34.

Copeland, Brian and Aaditya Mattoo (2008): "The Basic Economics of Services Trade", Aaditya Mattoo, Robert M. Stern and Gianni

Zanini (Eds), *A Handbook of International Trade in Services*, Oxford University Press, New York, USA, pp. 84-129.

Cowhey, Peter and Mikhail M. Klimenko (2004): "The New International Trade Regime in Telecommunication Services and Network", *Emerging Markets Finance and Trade*, Vol. 40, No. 1, pp. 59-94.

Damesick, Peter J. (1986): "Service Industries, Employment and Regional Development in Britain: A Review of Recent Trends and Issues", *Transactions of the Institute of British Geographers*, New Series, Vol. 11, No. 2, pp. 212-26.

Daniels, P.W. (2000), "Export of Services or Servicing Exports?", *Geografiska Annaler. Series B, Human Geography*, Vol. 82, No. 1, pp. 1-15.

De, P. (2006): "The Growth of International Trade in Services in Developing Countries: Some Implications", *Journal of International Logistics and Trade,* Vol. 4, No. 2, pp. 75-106.

De, Prabir and Ajitava Raychaudhuri (2008): "Is India's Services Trade Pro-Poor? A Simultaneous Approach", *Macro Regional Knowledge Hub,* Working Papers, No. 16.

Deodhar, Satish Y. (2002): "Educational Services for India in WTO Negotiations", *Economic and Political Weekly*, Vol. 37, No. 19, pp. 1791-95.

Dossani, Rafiq (2005): "Globalisation and the Off-Shoring of Services: The Case of India", *Off-Shoring White-Collar Work*, Brookings Institution Press, Washington DC, pp. 241-77.

Eichengreen, Barry and Poonam Gupta (2012): "Export of Services: Indian Experience in Perspective", Working Paper No. 102, National Institute of Public Finance and Policy, New Delhi, http://www.nipfp.org.in.

Eschenbach, Felix and Bernard Hoekman (2006): "Services Policy Reform and Economic Growth in Transition Economies", *Review of World Economics*, Vol. 142, No. 4, pp. 746-64.

Eusebio, R., J.L. Andreu, and M.P.L. Belbeze (2007): "Management Perception and Marketing Strategy in Export Performance", *Journal of Fashion Marketing and Management*, Vol. 11, No. 1, pp. 24-40.

Fink, Carsten and Deunden Nikomborirak (2007): "Rules of Origin in Services: A Case Study of Five ASEAN Countries", *Policy Research Working Paper No. 4130*, World Bank.

Fink, Carsten, Aaditya Mattoo and Ileana Cristina Neagu (2002): "Trade in International Maritime Services: How Much Does Policy Matter?", *The World Economic Review*, Vol. 16, No. 1, pp. 81-108.

Francois, Joseph and Bernard Hoekman (2010): "Services Trade and Policy", *Journal of Economic Literature*, Vol. 48, No. 3, pp. 642-92 URL: http://www.jstor.org/stable/20778764. Accessed: 06/01/2015, 03:38.

Francois, Joseph F. and Kenneth A. Reinert (1996): "The Role of Services in the Structure of Production and Trade: Stylized Facts from a Cross-Country Analysis", *Asia-Pacific Economic Review*, Vol. 2, No. 1, pp. 35-43.

Gabriele, Alberto (2004): "International Trade in Services and the Evolving Position of Developing Countries", *Journal of Economic Integration*, Vol. 19, No. 4, pp. 780-803.

Ghani, Ejaz (2010): *The Service Revolution in South Asia*, (Ed.), Oxford University Press, New York, USA.

GOI (2001): "Report of the Joint Committee on International Trade in Services" (Prasad Committee), *Department of Commerce*, Ministry of Commerce and Industry, New Delhi, India, April 2001.

GOI (2005): "Strategy Paper on the Telecom Sector", *Economic Division*, Department of Economic Affairs, Ministry of Finance, New Delhi, India.

GOI (2009): "Foreign Trade Policy" (27th August 2009—31st March 2014), *Department of Commerce*, Ministry of Commerce and Industry, Government of India, New Delhi, India (http://dgft.gov.in).

GOI (2013): Ministry of Commerce and Industry, Department of Commerce, Government of India, New Delhi, India (commerce.nic.in/trade/international_ta_current.asp).

Gordon, Jim and Poonam Gupta (2003): "A Tale of Two Giants: India's and China's Experience with Reform", *Paper prepared for the IMF-NCAER Conference*, November 14-16, New Delhi.

Hansda, S.K. (2001): "Sustainability of Services-led Growth: An Input-Output Analysis of Indian Economy", *RBI Occasional Working Paper*, Vol. 22, No. 1, 2 and 3.

Hansda, Sanjay Kumar. (2002): "Services Sector in the Indian Economy: A Status Report", *RBI Staff Studies, Department of Economic Analysis and Policy,* S.S. (DEAP): 1/2002, September, Mumbai.

Hill, T.P. (1977): "On Goods and Services", *Review of Income and Wealth*, Vol. 23, No. 4, pp. 315-38.

Hindley, Brian (1990): "Principles in Factor-Related Trade in Services", Messerlin, Patrick A., Sauvant, Karl P., eds. *The Uruguay Round: Services in the World Economy*, with contributions by Bela Balassa et al. Washington, D.C., World Bank, New York: United Nations Centre on Transnational Corporations, pp. 12-18.

Hindley, Brian and Smith, Alasdair (1984): "Comparative Advantage and Trade in Services", *World Economy*, Vol. 7, No. 4, pp. 369-89.

Hirsch, Seev (1989): "Services and Service Intensity in International Trade", *Review of World Economics*, Vol. 125, No. 1, pp. 45-60.

Hoekman, Bernard and Carlos Primo-Braga (1997): "Protection and Trade in Services: A Survey", *C.E.P.R. Discussion Papers*, CEPR Discussion Papers: 1705.

Holmes, Frank (1990): "ANZCERTA, Trade in Services and ASEAN", *ASEAN Economic Bulletin*, Vol. 7, No. 1, pp. 1-10.

Islam, Saiful and Parag Jafar Siddique (2014): "Revealed Comparative Advantage of Bangladeshi Leather Industry with Selected Asian Economies", *IOSR Journal of Business and Management,* Vol. 16, No. 12, pp. 44-51.

Jain, M.P. (1968): "Some Aspects of Indian Federalism", Accessed on 10/01/2015, (http://www.zaoerv.de), Vol. 28, No. 2, pp. 301-64.

Jain, Sunil and T.N. Ninan (2010): "Servicing India's GDP Growth", in Acharya, Shankar and Rakesh Mohan (eds.), "India's Economy: Performance and Challenges—Essays in Honour of Montek Singh Ahluwalia", Oxford University Press, pp. 328-65.

Javalgi, R.G. and Martin, C.L. (2007): "Internationalization of Services: Identifying the Building Blocks for Future Research", *Journal of Services Marketing*, Vol. 21, No. 6, pp. 391-97.

Joseph, K.J. and K.N. Harilal (2001): "Structure and Growth of India's IT Exports: Implications of an Export-Oriented Growth Strategy", *Economic and Political Weekly*, Vol. 36, No. 34, pp. 3263-70.

Kaminski, Bartlomiej; Zhen Kun Wang; L. Alan Winters; Andre Sapir and Iatvan P. Szekely (1996): "Exports Performance in Transition Economies", *Economic Policy*, Vol. 11, No. 23, pp. 421-42.

Kapur, Devesh; Ravi Ramamurti and Deependra Moitra (2001): "India's Emerging Competitive Advantage in Services", *The Academy of Management Executive (1993-2005)*, Vol. 15, No. 2, pp. 20-33.

Krugell, W. and M. Matthee (2009): "Measuring the Export Capability of South African Regions", *Development Southern Africa,* Vol. 26, No. 3, pp. 459-76.

Kumar, N. (1998): "Multinational Enterprises, Regional Economic Integration, and Export-Platform Production in the Host Countries: An Empirical Analysis for the US and Japanese Corporations", *Review of World Economics*, Vol. 134, No. 3, pp. 450-83.

Kumar, Nagesh (2001): "Indian Software Industry Development: International and National Perspective", *Economic and Political Weekly*, Vol. 36, No. 45, pp. 4278-90.

Kuźnar, Andżelika (2007): "*International Trade in Services in Developing Countries—Threats and Opportunities, Are Developing Countries Competitive?*" (http://www.etsg.org/ETSG2007/papers/kuznar.pdf), accessed on 06-12-2014 at 12.15 pm, pp. 1-16.

Lages, Luis Filipe and Cristiana Raquel Lages (2004): "The STEP scale: A Measure of Short-Term Export Performance Improvement", *Journal of International Marketing*, Vol. 12, No. 1, pp. 36-56.

Lages, Luis Filipe; G. Silva; and C. Styles (2009): "Relationship Capabilities, Quality, and Innovation as Determinants of

Export Performance", *Journal of International Marketing*, Vol. 17, No. 4, pp. 47-70.

Lages, Luis Filipe; Carmen Lages and Cristiana Raquel Lages (2005): "European Managers' Perspective of Export Performance Determinants", *Journal of Euro Marketing,* Vol. 15, No. 2, pp. 75-92, (http://www.haworthpress.com/web/JEM), Accessed: 07/01/2015, 03:00.

Langhammer, R. (2002): "Developing Countries as Exporters of Services: What Trade Statistics Suggest", *Journal of Economic Integration*, Vol. 17, No. 2, pp. 297-310.

Lee, C. and D.A. Griffith (2004): "The Marketing Strategy Performance Relationship in an Export-Driven Developing Economy", *Journal of International Marketing Review*, Vol. 21, No. 3, pp. 321-34.

Leonidou, L.C.; C.S. Katsikeas and S. Samiee (2002): "Marketing Strategy Determinates of Export Performance: A Meta-Analysis", *Journal of Business Research*, Vol. 55, No. 1, pp. 517-67.

Mahalanobis, P.C. (1953): "Some Observations on the Process of Growth of National Income", *Sankhya*, Vol. 12, No. 4, pp. 307-12.

Majeed, Muhammad Tariq; Eatzaz Ahmad and M. Idrees Khawaja (2006): "Determinants of Exports in Developing Countries", *The Pakistan Development Review*, Vol. 45, No. 4, pp. 1265-76.

Mavrogiannis, M.; M.A. Bourlakis; P.J. Dawson and R.N. Mitchell (2008): "Assessing Export Performance in the Greek Food and Beverage Industry", *Journal of British Food*, Vol. 110, No. 7, pp. 638-54.

Melvin, J.R. (1987): "Services: Dimensionality and Intermediation in Economic Analysis", *Institute for Research in Public Policy Discussion Paper*, January.

Melvin, J.R. (1989): "Trade in Producer Services: A Heckscher-Ohlin Approach", *Journal of Political Economy*, Vol. 95, No. 5, pp. 1180-96.

Moghaddam, Farshid Movaghar; Abu Bakar Bin Abdul Hamid; Siti Zaleha Abdul Rasid and Hassan Darestani (2011): "The Influence of Export Marketing Strategy Determinants on Firm Performance: A Review of Empirical Literatures Between 1993-2010", *International Journal of Fundamental Psychology and Social Sciences*, Vol. 1, No. 2, pp. 26-34.

Mukherjee, Arpita (2013): "The Service Sector in India", *ADB Economics Working Paper Series* No. 352, Asian Development Bank, Manila, Philippines, pp. 1-21.

Mukhopadhyay, Sukumar (2002): "Globalisation and Indian Services Sector", *Economic and Political Weekly*, Vol. 37, No. 40, pp. 4097-98.

Mzumara, Macleans; Anna Chingarande and Roseline Karambakuwa (2012): "An Analysis of Comparative Advantage and Intra-North American Free Trade Agreement (NAFTA) Trade Performance", *Journal of Sustainable Development*, Vol. 5, No. 11, pp. 103-17.

Nandi, Sukumar and Basudeb Biswas (1991): "Exports and Economic Growth in India: Empirical Evidence", *The Indian Economic Journal*, Vol. 38, No. 3, pp. 53-57.

Ogunmokun, Gabriel and Simone Ng (2004): "Factors Influencing Export Performance in International Marketing: A Study of Australian Firms", *International Journal of Management*, Vol. 21, No. 2, pp. 56-69.

Peterson, J. and R. Barras (1987): "Measuring International Competitiveness in Services", *The Service Industries Journal*, Vol. 7, No. 2, pp. 131-42.

Pfaffermayr, Michael (1996): "Foreign outward Direct Investment and Exports in Austrian Manufacturing: Substitutes or Complements?", *Weltwirtschaftliches Archiv*, Vol. 132, No. 2, pp. 501-22.

Polese, Mario and Roger Verreault (1989): "Trade in Information Services: How and Why Regions Develop Export Advantages", *Canadian Public Policy/Analyse de Politiques*, Vol. 15, No. 4, pp. 376-86.

Prasad, H.A.C. (2005): "Market Access for Exports from India: Issues for Post-Cancun WTO Negotiations in Industrial, Agricultural and Services Sectors", *Academy of Business Studies*, New Delhi (www.worldtradescanner.com).

Prasad, H.A.C. and R. Sathish (2010): "Policy for India's Services Sector", *Working Paper No. 1/2010-DEA, Department of Economic Affairs*, Ministry of Finance, Government of India, New Delhi.

Raipuria, Kalyan (2001): "Services Exports: "Knowledge Bowl Yet to Yield Major Gains", *Economic and Political Weekly*, Vol. 36, No. 35, pp. 3351-52.

Rakshit, Mahir (2007): "Services-Led Growth: The Indian Experience", *Money and Finance, ICAR Bulletin*, February, pp. 91-126.

Ray, Alok (1991): "Trade in Services for Developing Countries in 1990s: Problem and Prospects", *Economic and Political Weekly*, Vol. 26, No. 9/10, pp. 519-27.

Richards, D. (2001): "Exports as a Determinant of Long-run Growth in Paraguay, 1966-1996", *Journal of Development Studies*, Vol. 38, No. 1, pp. 128-46.

Saez, Sebastian and Arti Grover Goswami (2010): "Uncovering Developing Countries' Performance in Trade in Services", *World Bank*, Washington, DC. (https://openknowledge.worldbank.org/handle/10986/10141).

Sampson, Gary P. and Richard H. Snape (1985): "Identifying the Issues in Trade in Services", *World Economy*, Vol. 8, No. 2, pp. 171-82.

Sapir, A. and C. Winter (1994): "Services Trade", in D. Greenway and L. Winters (eds.), *Surveys in International Trade, Blackwell Economic Theory and the Role of Government in East Asian Industrialisation*, Princeton University Press, Princeton.

Scherrer, Christoph (2005): "GATS: Long-Term Strategy for the Commodification of Education", *Review of International Political Economy*, Vol. 12, No. 3, pp. 484-510.

Serin, V. and A. Civan (2008): "Revealed Comparative Advantage and Competitiveness: A Case Study for Turkey Towards the EU", *Journal of Economic and Social Research*, Vol. 10, No. 2, pp. 25-41.

Sharma, S. and D. Dhakal (1994): "Causal Analysis between Exports and Economic Growth in Developing Countries", *Applied Economics*, Vol. 26, No. 12, pp. 1145-57.

Sidhu, Gurkirpal Singh and Rakesh Jindal (2006): "Gats and Higher Education: India Moving Towards Global Markets", *The Indian Journal of Political Science*, Vol. 67, No. 2, pp. 381-96.

Singh, P.N. (2000): "India's International Trade in the Third Millennium", *Delhi Business Review,* Vol. 1, No. 2.

Spero, Joan Edelman (1983): "Trade in Services: Removing Barriers", *PS*, Vol. 16, No. 1, pp. 17-24, (www.jstore.org), Accessed: 04/01/2012, 01:36 PM.

Stern, R. and B. Hoekman (1988): "The Service Sector in Economic Structure and in International Transactions," in L. Castle and C. Findlay (eds.), *Pacific Trade in Services*, Sydney: Allen & Unwin.

Tantong, P.; K. Karande; A. Nair and A. Singhapakdi (2010): "The Effect of Product Adaptation and Market Orientation on Export Performance: A Survey of Thai Managers", *Journal of Marketing Theory and Practice*, Vol. 18, No. 2, pp. 155-70.

Teltscher, S. (2002): "Export Competitiveness and E-services", *E-Commerce and Development Report*, 2002, Part 2, Chapter 9, UNCTAD, Geneva, Switzerland.

Tharakan, P.K.M.; Ilke Van Beveren and Tom Van Ourti (2005): "Determinants of India's Software Exports and Goods Exports", *The Review of Economics and Statistics*, Vol. 87, No. 4, pp. 776-80.

UNCTAD (2004): "Exports of Services and Economic Growth in Developing Countries", *Division on International Goods and Services, and Commodities*, UNCTAD, Geneva, Switzerland.

United Nations (2002): "Manual on Statistics of International Trade in Services: EC, IMF, OECD, UNCTD and WTO", *Department of Economics and Social Affair, Statistic Division Services, Manual* No. 86, New York.

Vijayasri, G.V. (2013): "The Importance of International Trade in World", *International Journal of Marketing, Financial*

Services and Management Research, Vol. 2, No. 9, pp. 111-19.

Winsted, K.F. and P.G. Patterson (1998): "Internationalization of Services; The Service Exporting Decisions", *Journal of Services Marketing*, Vol. 12, No. 4, pp. 294-311.

Woodward, David (2005): "The GATS and Trade in Health Services: Implications for Health Care in Developing Countries", *Review of International Political Economy*, Vol. 12, No. 3, pp. 511-34.

World Bank (2004): "Sustaining India's Services Revolution: Access to Foreign Markets, Domestic Reform and International Negotiations", *Working Paper*, Reports No. 31795, Development Research Group (DECRG), Washington DC, World Bank.

World Economic Forum (2008): "The Global Competitiveness Report, 2008-09", Full Data Edition, *World Economic Forum*, Geneva, Switzerland.

World Economic Forum (2013): "The Global Competitiveness Report, 2013-14", Full Data Edition, *World Economic Forum*, Geneva, Switzerland.

WTO (2013): "International Trade Statistics 2013", *World Trade Organisation*, (www.wto.org), Accessed on 27/11/2014, 11 AM.

WTO (2014): "International Trade Statistics 2014", *World Trade Organisation,* (www.wto.org), Accessed on 27/11/2014, 11:15 AM.

❐